Case Studies in Health Care Ethics

Case Studies in
Health Care Ethics

TIMOTHY EVES

Copyright © 2019 by Soft Skills Power, LLC

All rights reserved.
Published in the United States by Soft Skills Power, LLC.

ISBN: 978-1-951366-02-5

Cover design copyright © 2019 by Soft Skills Power, LLC

Soft Skills Power, LLC
450 Lexington Avenue, #1479, New York, NY 10163
www.softskillspower.com

Printed in the United States of America

CONTENTS

PART 1: DOCTORS AND PATIENTS — p. 1
Case Study 1: Obesity — p. 3
Case Study 2: Barbie — p. 13
Case Study 3: "Please Let Me Die" — p. 19
Case Study 4: "I Don't Want It Done" — p. 25
Case Study 5: The *Tarasoff* Decision — p. 29
Case Study 6: Noble Lies — p. 33
Case Study 7: Jack Kevorkian — p. 37
Case Study 8: Terri Schiavo — p. 41

PART 2: PARENTS AND CHILDREN — p. 47
Case Study 9: Miss Sherri — p. 49
Case Study 10: *Roe v. Wade* — p. 53
Case Study 11: The Octomom — p. 57
Case Study 12: Baby M — p. 61
Case Study 13: Savior Sibling — p. 65
Case Study 14: Autism and Vaccination — p. 69
Case Study 15: Medical Science versus Christian Science — p. 75
Case Study 16: The Vegan Baby — p. 79

PART 3: RESEARCHERS AND SUBJECTS — p. 83
Case Study 17: Bad Blood — p. 85
Case Study 18: Prison Experiments — p. 91
Case Study 19: Huntington's Disease – and Beyond — p. 97
Case Study 20: The Baby and the Baboon — p. 101
Case Study 21: A Hundred Thousand Monkeys — p. 105
Case Study 22: "One of the Worst Things I Had Ever Done" — p. 109

PART 4: THE AMERICAN HEALTH CARE SYSTEM — p. 113
Case Study 23: A Hopelessly Flawed System? — p. 115
Case Study 24: Obamacare — p. 121

SOURCES AND FURTHER READING — p. 127

Part 1
DOCTORS AND PATIENTS

Case Study 1
Obesity

Maria

Maria is seventeen years old and obese – which is different from, and more serious than, being overweight. Whereas obesity is defined as having a body-mass index (BMI) of 30 or higher, overweight is defined as having a BMI of at least 25 but less than 30. People's BMI is determined by their height and weight. Someone who is 5' 3", as Maria is, is overweight if she weighs at least 141 lb. and is obese if she weighs at least 168 lb. Weighing 230 lb., Maria has a BMI of 41. She has just returned home from a snorkeling trip in the Florida Keys, where she experienced fatigue, nausea, and profound anxiety. Concerned, her mother takes her to a doctor. The doctor finds that, although Maria's liver and kidneys are functioning normally, her glucose and triglyceride levels are much too high: her glucose is 214 milligrams per deciliter (the normal range being between 70 and 100 milligrams per deciliter), while her triglycerides come in at 277 milligrams per deciliter (normal being less than 150 milligrams per deciliter). Upon examining the test results, the doctor concludes that Maria has type 2 diabetes.

Maria's problems stem from her childhood. Both of her parents – second-generation immigrants from Mexico – are overweight, and her mother's side of the family has a history of diabetes, hypertension, and heart disease. At birth, Maria was a heavier-than-average 10 lb. 6 oz., but, as is common among Hispanics, Maria's mother took her daughter's size to be a sign of strength and good health. During her early childhood, Maria enjoyed eating fresh fruits and rice and beans, and, observing her two older brothers eating American foods, she also became partial to pizza, chips, and soda. Because she was active, frequently playing outdoors all day with her brothers, Maria's pediatrician wasn't alarmed that her weight was in the 95th percentile, though he suggested that Maria's mother should monitor the girl's activity and food intake. Maria's mother, however, found the suggestion insulting, believing that an American doctor wouldn't know what's healthy for a Hispanic girl. She felt reassured when Maria started kindergarten, because she saw that several of Maria's classmates were also heavy and supposed this to be normal and healthy. In school, Maria made several new friends and continued to be an active and confident child.

About the time she started the fifth grade, Maria and her family moved from Tucson, Arizona, to Miami, Florida. For Maria, the transition was difficult. Noticing how slim many of her new classmates were, she became self-conscious about her weight for the first time. When she was invited to a beach party, she hesitated to go because she didn't want the other kids to see her in a bathing suit. She changed her mind, though, when her mother told her that she should be proud of her curves. At the party, the boys teased the girls by comparing them with different animals. Maria, they said, resembled a manatee. Although Maria hid her feelings, the remark devastated her.

Near the end of the eighth grade a semiformal dance was held. All the girls had a date for the dance – except Maria. In an attempt to comfort her, her father said that the boys simply didn't recognize her beauty yet, but Maria felt unattractive nonetheless. One day, when her mother caught her critically examining her body in the mirror, Maria exclaimed that she was fat and burst into tears. Seeing how low their daughter's self-esteem had become, Maria's parents took action. After consulting a dietitian, Maria's mother incorporated more fresh vegetables and fruits into the family's diet, and her father enrolled Maria in karate lessons with her older brothers. Maria enjoyed karate, and she lost weight – by the beginning of the ninth grade, her school uniforms had become too big for her to wear. She was happier than she had been in years.

Then disaster struck. Maria's father suffered from a stroke, which his doctors believed was caused by years of uncontrolled type 2 diabetes. Paralyzed on his right side and unable to speak, he could no longer do his job. Maria's brothers were now in college, and, to pay for the mounting medical bills, her mother took a job as a legal secretary. No longer able to afford luxuries, Maria was forced to abandon her karate lessons. She spent much of her time alone, watching TV or surfing the Internet, and she got her meals from fast-food restaurants near her home. She regained the weight she'd lost and became depressed. Her grades at school deteriorated. A couple of years later, during the summer before her senior year of high school, Maria joined some friends for snorkeling in the Florida Keys. That was when she became ill, and that was when she was diagnosed with type 2 diabetes.

Maria decides that she doesn't want to suffer the same fate as her father. She consults a dietitian and takes classes to help her better understand her condition and how best to manage it. Finding inspiration from a TV show about adolescents controlling their weight, she changes her diet and starts exercising daily. She even returns to her karate lessons. Within three months, she loses 15 lb. She is currently taking metformin and simvastatin, two medications commonly prescribed for diabetics, but she hopes to be free of all medications by her twentieth birthday.

Jim

Jim, an accountant for a large manufacturing firm, is twenty-five years old, 6' 5", and just under 400 lb., giving him a BMI of 47, well above the threshold for obesity. He's playing basketball with some friends. Although his weight slows him down, as does his knee, which he injured in a football game when he was in college, Jim plays the best he can. About an hour after the game starts, Jim is sweating profusely and feels dizzy. He experiences an odd sensation in his jaw, and a sharp pain shoots down his left arm. He tells his friends that it feels like an elephant is sitting on his chest. His friends call 9-1-1, and Jim is taken to a nearby hospital, where doctors confirm that he has just had a heart attack.

Jim's obesity, and his consequent health problems, like Maria's, has its origins in his childhood. Like Maria, Jim had a heavy father, who at 6' 0" weighed 350 lb. Like Maria, Jim was larger than average at birth, weighing 10 lb. 4 oz. Like Maria, he was praised as a baby for his strength and beauty. Like Maria, he maintained in his preschool years a weight in the 95th percentile, and enjoyed eating a variety of foods, including pizza, chips, and ham sandwiches, as well as apples, pears, and bananas. Like Maria, he was active in his early childhood, so that his pediatrician expressed little concern about his weight, merely advising his mother to watch his food intake and level of activity. Like Maria's mother, Jim's mother, offended by the pediatrician's advice, as it implied that Jim was "chubby," declined to take action.

When Jim started school, he was shy and made few friends. His classmates taunted him because of his weight. Rather than play with his classmates, Jim watched TV and played videogames, and he found solace in junk food, snacking on potato chips and drinking eight cans of soda a day. His grades went down and his weight went up, but family members reassured his parents that the weight gain was merely a phase or a growth spurt. Jim remained withdrawn until high school, when he played football as a defensive lineman. He excelled at the sport, drawing attention from college scouts. His parents were overjoyed that their son had at last found a way to fit in. During his senior year in high school, Jim was awarded a scholarship to play football for a Division I college. By the time he started college, he had reached his full height of 6' 5" and weighed 315 lb.

During the homecoming game of his sophomore year, Jim hyperextended his knee and tore his meniscus. The injury ended his football career. Although Jim continued with his studies and earned his Bachelor's degree, the time that he had been using to work out in the weight room and practice on the field was now used for partying. Jim drank large quantities of beer, and ate lots of pizza, nachos, and Buffalo wings. When he graduated from college at age twenty-four, he weighed 400 lb.

Now, a year later, Jim is lying in a hospital undergoing cardiac catheterization and angioplasty for his heart attack. His doctors discover that he also suffers from several other obesity-related maladies: type 2 diabetes, hyperlipidemia, hypertension, and mild kidney disease. Jim is little troubled by the bad news, because he believes that, being still young, he has ample time to make whatever lifestyle changes he needs to make. The result of his belief is that he delays making the necessary changes. He repeatedly misses doctors' appointments, and when he starts taking insulin he repeatedly misses doses. He doesn't monitor his diet, and he doesn't exercise when time permits. When he's told several years later that he's in the early stages of renal failure, he finally takes steps to improve his health, but a few weeks later he abandons these steps, reverting to his former bad habits. Shortly before his thirty-fourth birthday, he has another heart attack. The heart attack is mild, but the damage to his kidneys is so great that he is placed on hemodialysis three times a week. He can't maintain his job as an accountant and starts receiving Medicare and Medicaid to cover his health care costs. At the age of forty-two, he dies of a massive heart attack. At the time he dies, he is still on dialysis, he is blind, and he has a chronic open wound.

The Costs of Obesity

Jim and Maria aren't alone in their obesity. In the United States today, 39.8% of adults and 18.5% of children are obese. Among adults, Hispanics have the highest rate of obesity in the nation at 47.0%, with non-Hispanic blacks following close behind at 46.8%. The rate of obesity among non-Hispanic whites is 37.9%, and Asians fare best at 12.7%. Far more Americans are obese today than four decades ago: in 1980 only 17% of adults and 6% of children were obese.

The increase in obesity has implications for the health of Americans. As the stories of Jim and Maria make clear, obesity is causally related to a variety of disorders, including type 2 diabetes, blindness, kidney failure, stroke, heart disease, hypertension, and wounds that fail to heal. The monetary costs of obesity-related disorders are staggering. Every year, type 2 diabetes, which usually results from obesity, costs $327 billion in medical bills, disability payments, and lost productivity. For just one patient, hospitalization for stroke care costs on average $20,396, end stage kidney disease costs on average $89,000 a year, and limb amputation resulting from wounds that don't heal commonly costs between $30,000 and $60,000. On average, the annual medical costs for an obese person are $1,723 higher than for a person of normal weight.

Many of America's newly obese, being young, haven't yet developed type 2 diabetes or other obesity-related disorders. But in all likelihood they, like Jim and Maria, eventually will. Those who become proactive about their health will still, like Maria, face a hopeful future. Those who don't will likely face a fate similar to that of Jim. Depending on whether they choose to be more like Maria or more like Jim, the young of today could have a lower quality of life than the young of yesterday, and they could die at a younger age. Today Americans live on average 78.7 years. By some estimates, that average – thanks to obesity – could drop in the next generation by two to five years. If this happens, obesity will shorten the lifespans of today's young people to a greater extent than will cancer and coronary artery disease combined.

Suggestions for Curbing Obesity

Given the monetary and quality-of-life costs that come with obesity, what actions, if any, should be taken to lower obesity rates? Although in at least some cases – including, perhaps, Jim's and Maria's – obesity has a genetic component, in almost all cases weight can be controlled through proper diet and exercise. But getting people to eat better and exercise more is a daunting challenge. Maria is now taking diet and exercise seriously, but only after being diagnosed with type 2 diabetes and witnessing the debilitating effects of her father's stroke – and there's no guarantee that her lifestyle changes will become permanent.

She may yet end up like Jim, who, despite multiple heart attacks and other serious health problems, chose not to improve his diet and exercise. Clearly, curbing obesity will require a lot of hard work. Here are a few options:

1) *Provide information.* For many years, the U.S. government has required that nutrition labels – which include, for example, information about the calories, saturated fat, sodium, sugars, and vitamins in a specified serving – be placed on packages of foods sold in supermarkets. But more could be done, and one additional step was taken on May 7, 2018, when a provision of the Affordable Care Act, popularly known as Obamacare, took effect, requiring restaurants and other establishments that sell restaurant-type foods to include calorie information on their menus. The new law applies only to chains having twenty or more locations, and covers, for example, Starbucks, Domino's Pizza, and movie theaters. The hope is that consumers will make healthier decisions if they know, for instance, that a six-inch tuna salad sandwich at Subway contains 470 calories while a six-inch roast beef sandwich sold at the same establishment contains only 320 calories.

A further step that could be, but hasn't yet, been taken concerns information about serving sizes. The serving sizes that food manufacturers put on their nutrition labels are often much smaller than the amounts consumers actually eat. For example, while the nutrition label on a container of Breyers vanilla ice cream lists one serving as half a cup (130 calories), for most consumers one serving is one cup (260 calories). Similarly, Président Light Brie has *more* fat per serving – 4.5 grams as compared with 3.5 grams – than Président Wee Brie, even though Wee Brie, unlike Light Brie, isn't a low-fat cheese. How can this be? Because whereas the serving size provided on the package of Light Brie is 28 grams, the serving size provided on the package of Wee Brie is only 17.5 grams. In this way, the nutritional information that food manufacturers provide may mislead consumers. For this reason, some health care experts suggest that food manufacturers be required to list more realistic serving sizes on their nutrition labels. If people have more information, and more accurate information, about food and exercise, they might make more prudent choices, and so keep their weight under control.

2) *Instill healthy habits early in life.* Jim and Maria ate unhealthy foods even early in their lives, and Jim spent much of his childhood watching TV and playing videogames rather than being active outdoors. This

was because Jim's and Maria's parents failed to heed the advice of their child's pediatrician about monitoring their child's activity and food intake. If parents were encouraged, or required, to consult with dieticians or take classes on providing their children with proper nutrition and exercise, childhood obesity might decrease. In combination with this, legislation could be passed requiring schools to serve kids more nutritious lunches, offer more nutrition classes, increase time for recess and physical education, and increase the number of extracurricular sports. Admittedly, hiring more physical education teachers and sports coaches will cost money, but this cost may in the long run be more than offset by the resultant savings in health care costs. Another idea, adopted in 2003 by Arkansas and in subsequent years by several other states, is to require schools to send to parents not only their child's academic report card but also a weight report card.

3) Reward healthy behavior. In West Virginia, which has one of the highest obesity rates in the nation, Medicaid patients are invited to participate in a wellness program. Those who accept the invitation sign a pledge to "do my best to stay healthy." To do their best to stay healthy, they must attend "health improvement programs as directed," get regular checkups, take prescribed medications, and go to the emergency room only for an emergency such as a heart attack or stroke. If they do all this, they receive "enhanced benefits," including diabetes management, cardiac rehabilitation, and home visits from a nurse when needed. Medicaid patients who decline to participate in the wellness program don't receive the enhanced benefits. They get only the benefits that the federal government requires. In defense of the wellness program, a West Virginia commissioner of health services said, "We want to reach people before they get chronic and debilitating diseases that will keep them on Medicaid for the rest of their lives." If a wellness program like this had been available to Jim, perhaps he would have lived beyond the age of forty-two.

4) Discourage unhealthy behavior. Instead of offering a carrot, as West Virginia has opted to do, we might wield a stick. The stick might take any number of forms:
- Tax foods – for example, soft drinks and high-sugar cereals – that contribute to obesity, much as cigarettes are taxed.
- Outlaw trans fats as ingredients in food products, which the Food and Drug Administration (FDA) has now done.

- Limit the legally allowable amount of sodium in restaurant foods.
- Pass legislation penalizing employers who choose not to provide nutrition and fitness programs for their employees.
- Pass legislation requiring employees to keep their weight below a specified limit; if they don't, penalize them, or even terminate their employment.

Critical Evaluation

Possibly some of these suggestions, if implemented, won't curb obesity as intended, or, if they do, will come at too heavy a cost. Requiring food manufacturers to list realistic serving sizes, for example, might backfire. Some studies reveal that many consumers view a listed serving size as the amount people may healthily eat rather than the amount people in fact eat. Consequently, if food manufacturers increase serving sizes in an attempt to make them more realistic, consumers may interpret the increase as an endorsement and eat more rather than less, thus gaining rather than losing weight. Also problematic is terminating the employment of people like Jim, who don't keep their weight below a specified limit. Unemployment is a heavy burden to bear, and it may lead to depression, which in turn may lead to decreased activity, increased eating, and increased weight.

However, some philosophers, who are known as libertarians, reject all of the suggestions considered above, no matter how successful or unsuccessful they may be in curbing obesity. According to libertarians, liberty is a fundamental value – people should be free to do anything they wish, as long as they don't interfere with the like freedom of others. I should be free, for example, to eat unhealthy foods and live a sedentary lifestyle. If you disapprove, and if I'm willing to listen, you should similarly be free to try to persuade – but not compel – me to make healthier choices. But suppose that in the end I don't make healthier choices, and suppose that I later develop obesity-related disorders. Do I then have a right that others help me pay my medical bills? Not at all. Just as you shouldn't compel me to live a healthy lifestyle, so I shouldn't compel you to pay for my health care costs. Either kind of compulsion would infringe on somebody's rights, preventing people from living their own lives according to their own lights.

The problem with the suggestions listed above, according to libertarians, is that all of them infringe on people's right to liberty. The government, for example, shouldn't penalize employers who don't provide nutrition and fitness programs for their employees, because such penalties infringe on the liberty of employers. Neither should the government offer a wellness program, as West Virginia does, because doing so infringes on the liberty of the taxpayers who must pay for the wellness program, whether they support it or not. In like manner, insisting that schools increase time for physical education or send home weight report cards infringes on the liberty of educators, while mandating that food manufacturers and restaurants provide information about the foods they produce or serve infringes on the liberty of food manufacturers and restaurateurs. The government should never force food manufacturers, restaurateurs, educators, or employers to run their businesses as *it* thinks they should be run. If people don't like a business practice, they may choose not to associate with the business. If, for instance, people don't like that a restaurant provides no information about the nutritional value of the foods it serves, they may choose to dine elsewhere. But that, according to libertarians, is as far as anyone may go. Anything further is a violation of the rights of others.

So what's the best way to handle the health care problems that obesity poses? What's the best way to ensure that people don't become obese and develop type 2 diabetes and other obesity-related disorders, as Jim and Maria did? To what extent, if any, may the government limit the liberty of the individual – to choose an unhealthy lifestyle, or to run one's business – in order to combat obesity?

Case Study 2
Barbie

A Human Barbie Doll

In 2004 Jenny Lee appeared on *The Oprah Winfrey Show* to talk about her addiction to cosmetic surgery. Just twenty-eight years old, Jenny had already undergone twenty-six procedures – including several Botox injections, three rhinoplasties, three lip implants, cheek implants, veneers, two breast augmentations, two breast lifts, and liposuction on her arms, stomach, hips, thighs, and knees. The cost of all these procedures came to about $80,000, and her recovery from them involved considerable discomfort and interruption of her daily activities. Why did Jenny do it?

Jenny explained to Oprah that, even though people had told her when she was a girl how pretty she was and how much she looked like Julia Roberts, she nonetheless had long suffered from low self-esteem. When she got married, her husband repeatedly complained that her nose was too big and her breasts too small. The criticisms wore her down. To please her husband, she tried cosmetic surgery. Her relationship with her husband didn't improve, though, and despite having started a family together – Jenny had given birth to a daughter – the couple eventually divorced. Jenny married again, to a much more supportive husband, but she remained dissatisfied with the way she looked. She wanted a nose like Michael Jackson's, lips like Angelina Jolie's, a profile like Jennifer Lopez's, and a chin and jawline like Jennifer Aniston's. She underwent further cosmetic procedures, but was still dissatisfied – every time she looked in the mirror, a host of imagined imperfections stared back at her. Her nose didn't seem quite right, small wrinkles had formed around her eyes, and she disliked the stretch marks that were the result of her pregnancy. The pain of looking in the mirror became so great that she willingly, eagerly embraced the pain of yet further surgeries – hoping that, with the next surgery, she would finally be happy with her appearance. She told Oprah that cosmetic surgery was all she could think about and that, if she could, she would undergo surgery every day.

Ironically, instead of boosting her self-esteem, the surgeries only made Jenny feel worse about herself. Her appearance had changed so drastically that people who knew her as a teenager could no longer recognize her. Her friends, unable to understand her, asked her why she wanted to change herself. She had been so pretty when she was younger, her friends told her. Now, after all the surgeries, she looked fake, unnatural. Oprah, too, was puzzled. She bluntly stated that Jenny looked like Barbie – blonde and slim, like the doll, and not quite human. Jenny replied that others had said the same thing to her. She added that she wished she had never started the surgeries, and that she felt broken inside and needed to be fixed.

Seven years later, in 2011, Jenny made a second appearance on Oprah's show, in a segment called "Where Are They Now?" Since her first appearance, Jenny had undergone an additional thirty-three procedures – including a fourth rhinoplasty and a circumferential body lift – for a grand total of fifty-nine procedures. The rhinoplasty pleased Jenny, as she declared her nose now to be perfect, and the circumferential body lift was a birthday present to herself. She had tried to give up surgeries twice – once shortly after her initial appearance on *Oprah* and once again after she gave birth to her second child, another daughter, so that she could be a more attentive mother – but in both cases she soon returned to her obsession. She suffered a major blow to her self-esteem when she was diagnosed with fibromyalgia, a mysterious condition characterized by a continual dull ache throughout the body that can interfere with sleep and concentration, and is often associated with weight gain. Indeed, Jenny had a much fuller figure in 2011 than she'd had in 2004. For the first time in her life, she had no control over her body – neither plastic surgery nor any other procedure can cure fibromyalgia. It's even possible that her surgeries caused her condition – one of the possible causes of fibromyalgia is the physical trauma that comes with surgery. Fortunately, her husband reassured her that he loved her just as she was, and this helped. Jenny told Oprah that she was encouraging her daughters to stay away from cosmetic surgery when they grow up, and that she was telling them they should like themselves just as they are.

An American Obsession

A great many Americans turn to cosmetic procedures to enhance their appearance – even if few of them can boast having as many procedures as Jenny Lee. In 2018, 17.7 million cosmetic procedures were performed in the United States, up two percent from 2017. Most of these procedures, such as Botox injections, were minimally invasive. A smaller number, but still a very large number – 1.8 million of the 17.7 million procedures – were surgical. These procedures include many of the kinds of procedures Jenny underwent – breast augmentation, rhinoplasty, liposuction, and others. They don't include, however, reconstructive surgery, such as tumor removal or laceration repair – reconstructive surgery is in a category separate from cosmetic surgery.

The five most common cosmetic surgical procedures performed in 2018 were breast augmentation (313,000), liposuction (258,000), rhinoplasty (213,000), eyelid surgery (206,000), and tummy tuck (130,000). The most common age at which people underwent cosmetic procedures was between forty and fifty-four, though a significant number of people who opted for cosmetic procedures were even younger than Jenny was when she had her first procedure – 65,000 aged nineteen and under underwent a surgical procedure in 2018, while 162,000 underwent a minimally invasive procedure. As in previous years, there was a wide gender gap, with women undergoing 92% of procedures. Almost half of the people who underwent a procedure – 45% – were repeat customers, having undergone at least one procedure before.

A minimally invasive procedure tends to be less costly than a surgical procedure. For example, whereas a Botox injection costs on average $397, breast augmentation costs on average $3,824, liposuction $3,518, rhinoplasty $5,350, eyelid surgery $3,156, and a tummy tuck $6,253. In 2018 Americans spent more than $16.5 billion on cosmetic surgical and minimally invasive procedures combined, including nearly $3 billion on Botox injections and over $1 billion each on breast augmentations and rhinoplasties.

Is Something Wrong with Americans?

Utilitarianism is an ethical theory according to which I should in all my actions bring the greatest happiness for the greatest number. To determine, on this theory, whether I should get a nose job that will make me look more like Michael Jackson, I'd need to ask myself how much happiness, and how much unhappiness, the nose job will bring. How painful will the surgery be, how long will it take me to recover, and how satisfied will I be with the results? Will a nose job increase not only my happiness but also the happiness of others – my spouse, for example, who may or may not like my new nose, and my surgeon, who makes a living by reshaping noses? Moreover, will spending $5,350 on a new nose bring more happiness into the world than spending the money in some other way – say, replacing the battered old carpet in my living room with a hardwood floor, or donating the money for cancer research? If spending the money on a new nose will bring more happiness – to me and to others – than spending the money in some other way, then, according to utilitarianism, I ought to get the new nose. But if spending the money in some other way will bring more happiness, I should spend the money in some other way. The calculations are doubtless complex, but a powerful utilitarian case could be made that something is seriously wrong with the American obsession with cosmetic procedures.

First, we might charge that those who undergo cosmetic procedures are self-absorbed, concerned more about their own happiness than the happiness of others. Although Jenny Lee attempted to give up her procedures so that she could be an attentive mother to her newborn daughter, her abstinence didn't last – in the end, she placed herself above her child. The facts that cosmetic surgery was all she could think about and that she spent $80,000 on her first twenty-six procedures and tens of thousands more dollars on the next thirty-three also suggest that she was focused primarily on herself. She could have used all that money instead to help the homeless in her hometown or the starving poor overseas. Indeed, undergoing all those procedures didn't even increase her happiness. Perhaps she would have been happier had she spent the money helping others, or had she spent the money on a good psychotherapist. Of course, not all patients undergoing cosmetic procedures are as self-absorbed as Jenny Lee or suffer from serious psychological problems. Nonetheless, imagine all the good that could have been done with the $16.5 billion that Americans spent on cosmetic procedures in 2018.

Second, we might question how responsible some plastic surgeons are. In her interview with Oprah, Jenny Lee said nothing about her surgeons. Did they wonder why Jenny wanted so many procedures? Did they believe that yet another procedure would benefit her? Did they consider the possibility that she suffered from body dysmorphic disorder (BDD), a condition characterized by an obsession with imagined or slight imperfections in one's appearance? An estimated 15% of cosmetic surgery patients suffer from BDD. Such patients would benefit more from psychotherapy and antidepressants than from cosmetic surgery. Should plastic surgeons, then, require that their patients undergo a mental health screening before they perform surgery? While some plastic surgeons show appropriate concern for the mental health of their patients, others seem more concerned with making money, focusing on their own rather than their patients' happiness.

Third, we might question how responsible American society is. Noting that Americans who undergo cosmetic procedures are overwhelmingly women, many feminists have expressed the worry that lurking in the background might be a sexist society, one that promotes the happiness of men more than the happiness of women. Consider, for instance, the standards of beauty for women, as reflected in the modeling industry. A typical female supermodel stands between 5' 9" and 5' 11" and weighs between 110 and 130 lb., giving her a body-mass index (BMI) of 17 or 18, which is underweight. This contrasts with the average American woman, who is 5' 3.7" and 170.6 lb., which, yielding a BMI of 29.5, is almost obese. The feminists' concern is that many women feel pressure to conform to the standards of beauty, so that their decision to undergo cosmetic procedures is less than fully free. Feminists raise similar concerns about related industries, such as the weight-loss industry, which often target women in their advertising. Rather than undergo cosmetic procedures, perhaps women would be happier if American society were to adopt more realistic standards of beauty.

So what, if anything, should be done about cosmetic procedures? Is anything wrong with the people who undergo them, the doctors who perform them, or the culture that promotes them? Should Jenny Lee be allowed to undergo a sixtieth procedure?

Case Study 3
"Please Let Me Die"

Leaning back in a well-cushioned chair, Dax Cowart reminisced about his life, the good times as well as the bad. As a camera recorded him, he reached into his pants pocket – clumsily, because he had no fingers – and withdrew a handkerchief, which he dabbed around his artificial eye. His face was heavily scarred, and much of his ears were missing. He was blind, and his hearing was impaired. He felt pain every day. In spite of the many challenges he confronted in his daily routine, Dax told to the camera that he was happy to be alive. He had had a long and successful career as a lawyer, he enjoyed lecturing about the rights of patients, he had cultivated a circle of valued friends, and – although he had divorced twice – his third marriage, then in its second decade, was deeply fulfilling.

That was in 2012. Many years earlier, Dax had felt differently. In 1973, when he was just twenty-five years old, he was in a hospital with serious injuries, facing months of excruciating treatments and lifelong disability. The treatments were unbearable to him. Repeatedly, he told his doctors to stop them. His doctors, perplexed, replied that, if they did as he requested, he would die. He said that he preferred to die. His doctors, however, didn't want to see him die when they knew they could save him. So they refused his requests and treated him against his will. They thought that, after pulling him through, he would come to see that treating him was the right thing to do. In this, though, they were mistaken. For his entire life, until he died of cancer in 2019, he believed his doctors should have respected his wishes and allowed him to die.

Here is Dax's story.

The Accident

Don Cowart – which was Dax's name in 1973[1] – turned the key again, and again the car wouldn't start. He'd been turning the key for three or four minutes, and was afraid the battery would run down. His father was with him, having raised the hood of the car to check the carburetor. The car was parked near a bridge, in a low, shady spot on a hot summer day. Don and his father had driven there to look at a piece of land that they thought might be a good buy. Don's father was a real estate broker, and Don was working with him while he waited for an opening as a commercial airline pilot. He had learned how to fly an airplane when he joined the Air Force, had served during the war in Vietnam, and was now back home in east Texas.

Then came the moment that irrevocably changed Don's life. A blue spark leapt from the carburetor, and an explosion threw Don onto the passenger seat. Fire engulfed the car. Managing to get out of the car, Don started toward the woods, because that was the only place that wasn't on fire. But then he saw that the underbrush was so dense that he'd likely get trapped in it and perish there. Therefore, changing direction, he ran through three walls of fire. When he cleared the last wall, he dropped to the ground and rolled to put out the flames. Then he got up and ran down the road in search of help. As he ran, he noticed that his vision was blurred, and realized that the fire had burned his eyes. He continued to run until he heard a man's voice, and then he dropped to the ground once again.

The man was a farmer, who, hearing the explosion, came out to investigate. Seeing Don lying on the ground, the farmer said, "Oh, my God!" It was then that Don realized how serious his burns must have been. The farmer left to find Don's father, and, when he returned, Don asked him to get him a gun. The farmer asked Don why he wanted a gun. Don answered, "Can't you see I'm a dead man? I'm going to die anyway." Apologetically, the farmer said he couldn't do that.

The first ambulance to arrive picked up Don's father. At the time, Don's father was alive, but he died shortly after. When the second ambulance arrived, Don didn't want the paramedics to take him to the

---

[1] After he was well enough to leave the hospital, Dax would sometimes attend social gatherings. At these gatherings, he would hear what appeared to be his name, but often someone else was being addressed. It was difficult for Dax to tell, because he was blind and didn't hear too well, and "Don" is a common name that sounds similar to several other common names, such as "Ron" and "Dan." Changing his name to Dax solved this problem.

hospital. He just wanted to die, and the sooner the better. Ignoring his protests, the paramedics started to pick him up. Merely touching him, however, caused searing pain. Don asked them to lift him by his belt instead. Soon after, he arrived at a nearby hospital.

The Treatments

The cause of the accident, an investigation later determined, was a leak in a propane transmission line. So much gas had accumulated in the hollow where Don and his father had parked their car that not enough oxygen was available to start the car. When the carburetor emitted a spark, the gas caught fire. Rex Houston, a lawyer and friend of the Cowarts, launched a lawsuit against the owners of the propane transmission line. He worried about Don's repeated refusals of treatment because, if Don, having no wife or children depending on him, were to die, the lawsuit would likely net little money. As Houston recalled years later, "I had to have a living plaintiff."

Don's mother, too, worried about Don's repeated refusals of treatment. Losing her husband was painful enough. Losing her son as well would have been too much to bear. She believed that her son's desire to die would pass once he started to recover, so when Don's doctors asked her to sign the consent forms for Don's treatment – because Don himself wouldn't sign – she readily agreed. Don didn't blame his mother for signing, but he did disagree with her. *He* should have been the one to make those decisions, because it was *his* life and *his* body, not hers.

Don kept refusing treatments because they were too painful for too long. The worst of the treatments were the daily tankings. Don had suffered third degree burns over sixty-five percent of his body. To save his life, his doctors needed to kill the bacteria that kept growing in his wounds. To this end, they dunked Don in a tank of chlorinated water. The tankings, according to Don, were "like pouring alcohol on an open wound," and being lifted out of the water, where the nerves in the burned parts of his body were exposed to the cold air, was even more agonizing: "All I could do was scream at the top of my lungs until I would finally pass out with exhaustion. The tankings took place seven days a week – week after week after week."

The painkillers the doctors prescribed did little to ease Don's pain. The doctors chose not to give him more painkillers because they were concerned that Don might develop an addiction to them. Unfortunately, in 1973, doctors knew less about drug addiction than they do now. Doctors now know that the benefits of more painkillers for Don would have outweighed the risks. Don's doctors therefore should have given him more painkillers – but even if they had, the treatments would still have been extremely unpleasant, and they would still have lasted more than a year.

In 1974, Don's doctors asked Dr. Robert White, a psychiatrist, to examine Don. They hoped that Dr. White would determine that Don suffered from depression or a mental illness that rendered him incompetent to make decisions about his own treatments. Such a determination would have made it easier for Don's doctors to justify getting consent for Don's treatments from Don's mother rather than from Don. When Dr. White examined Don, however, he found that Don was intelligent, articulate, and of sound mind, and a second psychiatrist confirmed Dr. White's conclusions. Dr. White made a twenty-nine minute video, called "Please Let Me Die," in which Don stated calmly that he wanted to die and argued forcefully that his doctors should allow him to do so.

Dr. White's conclusions and the video he made didn't deter Don's doctors. They continued to treat Don against his wishes. Eventually, Don was well enough to leave the hospital, but he had difficulty adapting to life with serious disabilities. On multiple occasions, he attempted suicide. Once, for example, he took an overdose of pills, but was discovered in time to have his stomach pumped. On another occasion, he crawled onto the middle of a highway, hoping that a truck would run him over, to no avail. In the end, he decided to live.

Critical Evaluation

A libertarian would agree with Dax's position, arguing that the doctors should have allowed him to die because forcing treatment on him interfered with his right to liberty. Dax himself explicitly advanced this libertarian argument when he said, "The individual freedom of a competent adult should never be restricted, except when it conflicts with the freedom of some other individual."

A utilitarian, by contrast, may or may not agree with Dax's position. On the one hand, had Dax been allowed to die, he wouldn't have endured the intense and prolonged suffering that his treatments caused, nor would he be in pain today. From a utilitarian perspective, this is good. On the other hand, if Dax had died, he would have missed out on a lot of happiness: the satisfaction of being a lawyer, the joy of close friendships, etc. Other people, too, would have missed out on happiness: his mother, his friends, his current wife, etc. A utilitarian would weigh all of this happiness against all of the pain and see which is greater. Which is greater, however, may be less than obvious.

A third perspective is also worth considering – Kantian ethics, which gets its name from the philosopher, Immanuel Kant, who founded it. According to Kant, the supreme principle of morality is neither to maximize individual liberty, as libertarians claim, nor to maximize overall happiness, as utilitarians believe. Instead, it's to treat persons always as ends and never as mere means. Kant believes that all persons have intrinsic value and, as such, should be treated with respect – or, in Kant's language, as ends. Persons, he says, are different from things. Things – such as a hammer or pencil – have only instrumental value, not intrinsic value. In other words, we may use them as mere means to achieve whatever ends we like. We may use a hammer as a means to build a house; we may use a pencil as a means to write a grocery list. As things, neither the hammer nor the pencil can ever be wronged. Persons, though, can be wronged, and we should never use them as mere means to achieve the ends we desire. We shouldn't, for example, kill our rich aunt as a means to getting our inheritance, and we shouldn't steal our neighbor's lawnmower as a means to getting our lawn mowed. We shouldn't do such things because persons have a dignity that things lack.

According to Kant, not only can we wrong *others* by treating them as mere means, but we can also wrong *ourselves* by treating ourselves as mere means. Drug addicts, for instance, use themselves as mere means to getting their next high, and prostitutes use their bodies as mere means to making money. Neither drug addicts nor prostitutes, in Kant's view, respect themselves. Kant would similarly claim that, by asking his doctors to let him die and by attempting suicide on multiple occasions, Dax treated himself as a mere means, and didn't respect himself. Committing suicide, Kant held, is morally wrong:

> As regards the concept of necessary duty to oneself, the man who contemplates suicide will ask himself whether his action can be consistent with the idea of humanity as an end in itself. If he destroys himself in order to escape from a difficult situation, then he is making use of his person merely as a means so as to maintain a tolerable condition till the end of his life. Man, however, is not a thing and hence is not something to be used merely as a means; he must in all his actions always be regarded as an end in himself. Therefore, I cannot dispose of man in my own person by mutilating, damaging, or killing him.

Should Dax have asked his doctors to let him die? Should his doctors have acceded to his request? Which ethical theory – libertarianism, utilitarianism, or Kantian ethics – provides the best analysis of what Dax and his doctors should have done?

Case Study 4
"I Don't Want It Done"

Tuesday, June 9, 1987

Angela Carder is about twenty-five weeks into her first pregnancy. The previous twenty-four weeks proceeded without incident, but now Carder is experiencing back pain and is having difficulty breathing. Concerned, she sees one of her doctors at George Washington University Hospital. The X-ray that the doctor orders reveals the worst news imaginable: cancer has almost completely infiltrated Carder's right lung.

This is not the first time Carder has had to battle cancer. She had cancer when she was thirteen, and again when she was twenty-three. Both times she endured months of chemotherapy and radiation, some of it experimental, and the second time she had to have her left leg and hip removed. But in the end she survived – on both occasions the cancer was driven into remission.

Then at age twenty-seven Carder married. She and her husband wanted to have children, but, given Carder's history of cancer and her missing leg and hip, the couple were unsure whether pregnancy would pose undue risks, and so before proceeding they consulted with Carder's physicians. Her physicians, agreeing that the risks were acceptable, gave Carder and her husband the go-ahead. Soon after, Carder was pregnant.

Now, however, diagnosed with cancer for the third time, Carder faces an uncertain and difficult future – and so does her unborn child.

Thursday, June 11

Carder is admitted to George Washington University Hospital as a patient. She knows that her cancer is at an advanced stage and that it's inoperable. She doesn't yet know whether she'll be able to beat cancer for a third time, and she doesn't yet know how the cancer will affect her pregnancy.

Friday, June 12

Carder feels better than she has for the past few days. When she is asked whether, given her condition, she would like to have the baby, she says she does.

Monday, June 15

Carder's health has deteriorated markedly. Her doctors inform her that her cancer is terminal. Moreover, she won't live long enough to deliver her baby at full term, which is still fourteen weeks away. Should she, then, have a Caesarean section now, twenty-six weeks into her pregnancy? Most twenty-six-week-old fetuses are viable – that is, they can be removed from the womb and survive with the aid of respirators and other machinery. But Carder's baby, growing inside a mother who has advanced cancer, isn't like most fetuses. According to the doctors, the baby will have a much better chance of surviving, perhaps an eighty percent chance, if Carder waits two more weeks and has a Caesarean section when the fetus is twenty-eight weeks old. By then the baby's lungs will be much better developed. Carder consents to this plan, and requests that for the next two weeks she be given palliative care. She understands that the medication she will need to control her pain and help her live two more weeks could impact the health of her baby. When she is asked if she would still like to have the baby, she answers with ambivalence: "I don't know, I think so."

Later in the day, as her health continues to deteriorate, Carder agrees to be intubated to help her breathe. Because of the breathing tube, and the sedatives she is given to control her pain, she is no longer able to communicate.

Tuesday, June 16

It's now clear that Carder will die within the next couple of days – she's not going to make it to the twenty-eighth week of her pregnancy, the time she had planned to have a Caesarean section. Under these new circumstances, the prospects for the fetus aren't promising, but it will have its best chance of surviving if a Caesarean section is performed immediately. However, performing a Caesarean section immediately will likely shorten Carder's life and cause her additional discomfort. Moreover, Carder consented to a Caesarean section only at twenty-eight weeks. She never indicated what she'd want if she were unable to live that long. Her doctors could reduce her medication, thereby allowing her to regain consciousness, and they could then ask her whether she would consent to an immediate Caesarean section. But they're reluctant to take this course of action, because reducing her medication could shorten her life. According to Carder's husband and parents, Carder would not want a Caesarean section under current circumstances, and for this reason they oppose the procedure. Carder's doctors decide to respect the wishes of the family.

When the hospital's administrators learn what has transpired, they contact a court, asking it to render a decision about whether a Caesarean section should be immediately performed. The administrators are concerned that, if Carder's fetus is allowed to die, those who support fetal rights might sue the hospital. But if the hospital carries out whatever decision a court reaches, the hospital won't be legally liable. The court agrees to intervene.

Judge Emmet G. Sullivan arrives at the hospital to ascertain the facts of the case. Present are Carder's husband and parents, as well as lawyers representing Carder, Carder's fetus, the hospital, and the ACLU. Dr. Hamner and Dr. Weingold, two of Carder's physicians, testify, as does a neonatologist, Dr. Edwards, who is not one of Carder's physicians. After listening to the testimony, Judge Sullivan concludes that the relevant facts are these:

1. Carder will die within the next twenty-four to forty-eight hours.
2. The fetus, according to Dr. Edwards, has a fifty to sixty percent chance of surviving if a Caesarean section is performed immediately.
3. The state has an important and legitimate interest in protecting viable fetuses.
4. While a Caesarean section could hasten Carder's death, any delay would decrease the fetus' chances of survival.
5. Carder's views on the matter are unknown.

In light of these facts, Judge Sullivan orders an immediate Caesarean section.

Dr. Hamner relays the judge's decision to Carder, who has regained consciousness, and then returns to the judge with this message: "I explained to her essentially what was going on.... I said it's been deemed we should intervene on behalf of the baby by Caesarean section and it would give it the only possible chance of it living. Would you agree to this procedure? She said yes. I said, do you realize that you may not survive the surgical procedure? She said yes. And I repeated the two questions to her again [and] asked her did she understand. She said yes."

Judge Sullivan sends Dr. Hamner back to Carder's room, along with Dr. Weingold and Carder's husband and mother, to confirm that Carder has consented to the surgery. Though still on medication, Carder is conscious. She can respond to questions, but, with a breathing tube in her windpipe, she can only nod and mouth words. When Dr. Hamner asks her whether she consents to the surgery, both he and Dr. Weingold clearly make out the words she mouths over and over: "I don't want it done."

When Drs. Hamner and Weingold report to the judge what they heard, the judge maintains that Carder's views are still unclear, because her medication may have prevented her from understanding questions and because the presence of family members, who were emotional, may have influenced her. Once again the judge orders an immediate Caesarean section. The lawyers representing Carder and the ACLU make an emergency appeal, but the three-judge panel that hears the appeal unanimously supports Judge Sullivan's decision. Despite the court's order, Carder's doctors refuse to perform the surgery, on the grounds that neither Carder nor her family consented to it. The hospital seeks out another doctor who is willing to perform the surgery and eventually finds one.

Angela Carder undergoes a Caesarean section. Within two and a half hours of being born, the baby – a girl – is dead. Carder regains consciousness long enough to be informed of her child's fate, and she cries. Soon after, she slips into a coma, and two days later she also is dead.

April 26, 1990

The District of Columbia Court of Appeals overturns Judge Sullivan's decision, arguing that the decision violated Carder's right to informed consent and her right to bodily integrity. It's three years too late for Carder, but the ruling is nonetheless important, having implications for the future. Because of the ruling, no one will ever have to go through what Angela Carder went through.

Should Judge Sullivan's decision have been overturned? Were Angela Carder's rights violated? If the Caesarean section hadn't been performed, would the rights of Carder's fetus have been violated? How should we weigh the rights of a fetus against the rights of its mother?

Case Study 5
The *Tarasoff* Decision

In 1967 Prosenjit Poddar left India, his home country, to study naval architecture at the University of California at Berkeley. His first year in the United States passed by without incident. Then in the fall of 1968, while taking a class on folk dancing at the university's International House, he met Tatiana Tarasoff. The two students got to know each other, and on New Year's Eve Tarasoff kissed Poddar. Assuming that the kiss was an expression of deep feelings for him, Poddar, who'd been smitten with Tarasoff from the moment he saw her, proclaimed his love for her. Tarasoff, however, rejected him. The kiss, she told him, was meant only as a sign of friendship – she had no interest in a romantic relationship with Poddar.

Poddar didn't take the rejection well. He became depressed and neglected his studies. At times his speech was disjointed. During the spring of 1969, he occasionally saw Tarasoff. Without her knowledge, he taped their conversations. He did so hoping to understand why she didn't return his love for her.

That summer Tarasoff studied in Brazil. While she was abroad, Poddar sought help at Cowell Memorial Hospital, a medical facility affiliated with the University of California at Berkeley. His psychotherapist was Dr. Lawrence Moore. In August, in a session with Moore, Poddar revealed that he intended to kill Tarasoff when she came back from Brazil. Moore took the threat seriously. After consulting with two of his colleagues, both of whom recommended that Poddar be committed involuntarily to the hospital's psychiatric unit, Moore contacted the university police. He told the police to bring Poddar to the hospital for involuntary commitment. He also told them that, although Poddar sometimes appeared rational, he suffered from paranoid schizophrenia and represented a danger to others.

The police spoke with Poddar. Poddar appeared to be rational and promised that he would stay away from Tarasoff. The police let him go. When Dr. Harvey Powelson, director of the clinic where Moore had treated Poddar, heard that the police had let Poddar go, he ordered that no further attempts be made to have Poddar committed involuntarily. For his part, Poddar, after his encounter with the police, immediately stopped his therapy with Moore.

Tarasoff returned to California for the fall semester. Nobody informed her, or her family, of Poddar's threat to kill her. Poddar persuaded Tarasoff's brother to share an apartment one block from Tarasoff's home. On October 27, 1969, Poddar tried to speak with Tarasoff at her home. She refused to speak with him. Poddar shot her with a pellet gun. She ran from her home, but Poddar chased after her and caught her. He stabbed her repeatedly and then returned to Tarasoff's home, where he called the police and waited for them to arrive. Tarasoff died of her injuries.

Poddar was found guilty of second-degree murder, but the conviction was overturned because the judge had failed to provide the jury with proper instructions. Rather than retry Poddar, the state of California released him on condition that he return to India. Poddar was a free man.

Unable to see justice done to Poddar, Tarasoff's parents sued the Regents of the University of California. They argued that the therapists responsible for Poddar's care didn't do enough to prevent their daughter's death. In the first place, they should have made further attempts, after the police let Poddar go, to confine Poddar. In the second place, they should have warned Tarasoff that Poddar had threatened to kill her. In short, according to the plaintiffs, Drs. Powelson, Moore, and others were negligent in their duties.

The case eventually reached the California Supreme Court. The court rejected the plaintiffs' first contention: the therapists responsible for Poddar's care were not legally liable for failing to confine Poddar. The reason was that the therapists were public employees, and a statutory provision – Government Code section 856 – shielded public employees from legal liability for failing to confine patients for mental illness.

The plaintiffs' second contention – that the therapists responsible for Poddar's care should have warned Tarasoff – was more difficult to evaluate. On the one hand, warning Tarasoff would have allowed her to protect herself from Poddar. If Tarasoff knew that Poddar had threatened to kill her, she might never have died. But on the other hand, warning Tarasoff would have been a breach of patient confidentiality. To receive appropriate treatment, a patient – especially a psychiatric patient – needs to share personal information with his doctor. But if he knows that his doctor won't keep personal information confidential, he won't be as likely to share personal information. His health could suffer as a result.

Which, then, is more important: protecting patient confidentiality or protecting potential victims? The California Supreme Court came down on the side of protecting potential victims. As the court put it, "The public policy favoring protection of the confidential character of patient-psychotherapist communications must yield to the extent to which disclosure is essential to avert danger to others. The protective privilege ends where the public peril begins." For this reason, the court ruled in favor of Tarasoff's parents.

The court's decision, reached in 1976, remains controversial even today. Many therapists argue, for example, that, far from protecting potential victims, as it was meant to do, the *Tarasoff* decision may put potential victims at greater risk. Thanks to the *Tarasoff* decision, therapists in California are now sometimes legally required to breach patient confidentiality. To avoid lawsuits, therapists may be more likely to refuse to treat potentially violent patients; to avoid dissemination of their personal information, potentially violent patients may be more likely to refuse either to seek help or, if they do seek help, to disclose their potential violence to their therapists. In consequence, potentially violent patients may be less likely to receive appropriate treatment and may therefore be more likely to commit acts of violence.

Did the California Supreme Court hand down the right decision? Does its decision save lives, or does it put more lives at risk?

Postscript: Around the time that the California Supreme Court reached its decision, law professor Alan Stone contacted Prosenjit Poddar. Seven years had passed since Poddar had killed Tarasoff. He was still living in India, and he reported that he was happily married.

Case Study 6
Noble Lies

Bus Stop

Hermann Schmidt sat at the bus stop just outside the Benrath Senior Center in Düsseldorf, Germany. He was a resident of the senior center, eighty-four years old and suffering from dementia. His short-term memory was almost completely nonfunctional, but he still had memories from long ago. He knew, for instance, that he used to be a professor of mathematics at the University of Düsseldorf, and that he had gotten married and raised four children, three girls and a boy. His wife, Emma, died two years ago of pancreatic cancer, but Professor Schmidt, as the staff at the senior center called him, didn't remember this.

Hannah König, who worked at the senior center, spotted Professor Schmidt at the bus stop. Sitting down next to him, she smiled and said, "Good morning, Professor. Nice day for a trip, isn't it?"

"Yes," Professor Schmidt replied curtly. "It's a nice day."

"Where are you going?" Hannah asked.

"Home. I'm going home. I want to be with my wife."

Hannah knew that Professor Schmidt's wife was dead, but she didn't say so. Many patients with dementia falsely believed that loved ones were still alive. In Hannah's view, setting the record straight – telling the professor, "I'm sorry, but your wife is dead" – would be cruel, as it would only induce a fresh round of grief. It was far better, she thought, to play along. Just the other day, for example, Professor Schmidt had asked her four times where his wife was. Each time he asked, she made something up. "Emma is out shopping. She should be back soon," she said one time. It was a lie, but it was also an act of mercy.

Today, however, Hannah didn't say anything about the professor's wife. Instead, she said, "You know, the bus won't be coming for a while yet. Why don't you join me for a cup of coffee, and then come back to the bus stop?"

Professor Schmidt peered at Hannah with suspicion. "Are you sure I've got time for coffee? I don't want to miss the bus."

"Yes," Hannah replied. "The bus won't be coming for another forty-five minutes. You have plenty of time!" This, too, was a lie. No bus would be coming in forty-five minutes. No bus would *ever* be coming. The bus stop, as Hannah well knew, was fake. The director of Benrath Senior Center had it installed because, as long experience showed, patients with dementia often wandered from senior centers and nursing homes in an attempt to return home and were later found at bus stops. Bus stops were attractive to the patients because they remembered taking buses home when they were younger. The fake bus stop proved effective – the staff at the senior center found many of their patients there, where it was easy to collect them and bring them back where they could be cared for.

Professor Schmidt paused for a moment, but in the end agreed. "All right," he said. "A cup of coffee might hit the spot."

Hannah brought the professor inside the senior center for his coffee. Five minutes later, the professor forgot that he had wanted to go home to be with his wife. In this way, Hannah was able to persuade him to return to the living quarters he had been assigned at the center.

The Ethics of Deception

Benrath Senior Center built its fake bus stop in 2008. Since then, other senior centers in Germany have followed suit. Nor is such deception confined to Germany. For example, the Lantern, a dementia care facility in Chagrin Valley, Ohio, has the appearance of a small Midwestern town from the 1940s, when most of its residents were children. The old-fashioned look – complete with façades that look like clapboard houses, a carpet of different shades of green that resembles growing grass, and a fake hardware store and oil company – is familiar, and hence comforting, to the residents. Deceptions such as these have met with broad approval. According to one survey, 70% of doctors who specialize in dementia care, and nearly 100% of care staff, admit that they sometimes lie to their patients.

Plato, too, would approve. According to Plato, people lie for two sorts of reasons. Sometimes, people lie because they believe that lying is in their own interest. This would happen, for example, if, in an attempt to make more money, a doctor tells a patient that a more expensive treatment is the most effective when she knows that, in fact, a less expensive treatment is equally effective. Plato agrees that this sort of lying – lying that takes advantage of others for one's own selfish purposes – is morally wrong. Sometimes, however, people lie, not for selfish reasons, but for a greater good, aiming to benefit others. This is the kind of lie that most specialists in dementia care tell. Hannah lied to Professor Schmidt for his sake, not hers; the fake bus stop aims to benefit the residents of the senior center, not its owners. This is also the kind of lie that Plato believes is morally right. He calls such lies "noble lies."

Not all philosophers, however, agree with Plato. Some argue that lying to patients, even when it's for their sake, tends to bring negative consequences – for the patients, for the lying health care professional, and for others.

1) Patients. The progress of dementia is unpredictable. Especially when it's in its early or middle stages, patients experience moments of lucidity. Thus, if Hannah tells Professor Schmidt that his wife is shopping and Professor Schmidt, in a moment of lucidity, remembers that his wife is dead, he may stop trusting Hannah. Similarly, he may stop trusting Hannah if he asks one of Hannah's coworkers where his wife is and the coworker tells a conflicting lie – for example, Hannah says, "Emma is out shopping," while the coworker says, "Emma is at home babysitting the grandkids." To be sure, Professor Schmidt may later forget that Hannah lied to him, but, even if he does, the feeling of mistrust may remain. Under these circumstances, caring for Professor Schmidt will likely become more difficult.

2) The lying health care professional. Lying, even the noble kind, often negatively affects the character and reputation of the liar. As the philosopher Sissela Bok suggests, of all the effects of lying, this one can be the most damaging: "What am I doing to myself if I do this over and over? If lying becomes a habit? Will I start doing it when I don't need to? And, if I start doing it with one [patient], why not with others?" According to Bok, lying, like violence, is an attempt to control others, to exert power over them, and power, as we know, can corrupt the one who holds the power.

3) Others. Lying can affect others, too. Suppose, for instance, that Professor Schmidt's young grandchildren, while visiting him at the senior center, notice that the bus stop is fake and hear Hannah lying to their grandfather. The grandchildren may themselves become more likely to lie, and they may not be able to distinguish the senior center's noble lies from less noble, more selfish lies. Bok puts the point this way: "As lies spread – by imitation, or in retaliation, or to forestall suspected detection – trust is damaged. Yet trust is a social good to be

protected just as much as the air we breathe or the water we drink....
When it is destroyed, societies falter and collapse."

All of these arguments suggest that lying to patients is wrong because doing so tends to have bad consequences. Some philosophers, however, believe that the rightness or wrongness of an action has nothing to do with its consequences. According to these philosophers, lying to patients may be wrong even if it has good consequences. What makes it wrong, they may argue, is that it treats patients as if they were things. Just as we use a pot to boil water or a hammer to pound nails, when we lie to patients, we use them as mere means to some desired end. Even if the end is noble, such as keeping the patients as happy and healthy as possible, we still treat them as if they were things. Patients, however, aren't things. They're people, endowed with a dignity and intrinsic value that pots and hammers lack. As such, they deserve our respect. Telling them the truth shows them this respect, honoring their dignity and intrinsic value. Lying to them, by contrast, shows disrespect, disregarding their dignity and intrinsic value. This is so no matter how painful the truth, or how beneficial the lie.

So is Plato right, or is he wrong? Should health care professionals ever lie to their patients? Is the fake bus stop at Benrath Senior Center a good idea, or should it be dismantled?

Case Study 7
Jack Kevorkian

Fifty-two-year-old Thomas Youk wanted to die. Having reached the advanced stages of amyotrophic lateral sclerosis (ALS), also known as Lou Gehrig's disease, Youk couldn't move his legs at all and he could only barely move his left arm. Speaking was difficult – he could utter no more than a few syllables at a time. Worst of all, he was unable to swallow. The thought of choking to death on his own saliva terrified him. With the approval of his wife and family, he contacted Dr. Jack Kevorkian.

Born in 1928 in Pontiac, Michigan, Kevorkian was a pathologist, oil painter, and jazz musician. From the earliest days of his medical career, he exhibited a fascination with death. During his residency at the University of Michigan hospital, for example, he photographed the eyes of dying patients. His aim in doing this was to help doctors be better able to tell when a patient was dead rather than merely unconscious or comatose, so they would know when and when not to attempt resuscitation. Later, in an article he published in 1959, he defended the use of death row inmates in medical research: "I propose that a prisoner condemned to death by due process of law be allowed to submit, by his own free choice, to medical experimentation under complete anesthesia (at the time appointed for administering the penalty) as a form of execution in lieu of conventional methods prescribed by law." Also early in his career, he attempted to persuade the Pentagon, based on research he had conducted, to use the blood of corpses, when no blood banks were available, to transfuse injured soldiers. None of these ideas ever took off.

In the 1980s Kevorkian turned his attention to assisted suicide. Initially, he merely advocated the practice; then in 1990 he helped Janet Adkins, a fifty-four-year-old woman who had been diagnosed the year before with Alzheimer's disease, to end her life. He attached her to a machine he called the Thanatron, which he devised himself. Adkins then administered to herself first a painkiller and then a poison that stopped her heart. The State of Michigan charged Kevorkian with murder, but the charge was dropped because Michigan had no law on assisted suicide.

Over the next eight years, Kevorkian reportedly helped 130 patients die. The State of Michigan, which, for the express purpose of stopping Kevorkian, had revoked Kevorkian's medical license and passed a law against assisted suicide, brought Kevorkian to trial four times. The first three times, however, Kevorkian was acquitted, and the fourth case ended in a mistrial. Jurors in these cases saw Kevorkian not as a murderer but as someone who wanted to end people's suffering. According to one juror, "He convinced us he was not a murderer, that he was really trying to help people out." Another juror said, "I don't feel it's our obligation to choose for someone else how much pain and suffering they can go through. That's between them and their God."

Emboldened by his victories, Kevorkian decided to shift from assisted suicide to euthanasia. In cases of assisted suicide, the doctor sets things up, but the person who performs the act that causes the patient's death is the *patient*. By contrast, in cases of euthanasia, the person who performs the act that causes the patient's death is the *doctor*. Kevorkian argued that euthanasia is preferable to assisted suicide because, having training in medicine, the doctor is better able to bring about a painless death than is the patient.

Accordingly, when he met Thomas Youk in 1998, Kevorkian proposed euthanasia. Youk accepted the proposal. On September 17 Kevorkian gave Youk three injections. The first put Youk to sleep; the second caused him to stop breathing; the third caused his heart to stop beating. Youk died quickly and, according to Kevorkian, painlessly. Kevorkian videotaped Youk's death and sent the tape to the CBS news program *60 Minutes*. *60 Minutes* aired excerpts of the tape on November 22.

Three days later, Kevorkian was charged with murder, and on April 13, 1999, after a two-day trial, the jury found him guilty of second-degree murder. Judge Jessica Cooper sentenced him to prison for ten to twenty-five years, with the possibility of parole. He was eventually released from prison in 2007 for good behavior. One of the terms of his parole was that he promise not to participate in any more assisted suicides or any more acts of euthanasia.

Was Kevorkian's sentence fair? Is anything wrong with assisted suicide? Is anything wrong with euthanasia? Should assisted suicide and euthanasia be legal?

Postscript: After his release, Kevorkian kept his parole promise, but he continued to argue in support of assisted suicide and euthanasia. In 2008 he ran as an independent candidate for United States Congress in Michigan, but won only 2.6 percent of the vote. In 2010 HBO broadcast a movie about him, *You Don't Know Jack*, featuring Al Pacino as the title character. Kevorkian died on June 3, 2011, at age eighty-three, after years of kidney problems. He didn't commit suicide and he wasn't euthanized, but according to his attorney, Mayer Morganroth, his death was painless.

Case Study 8
Terri Schiavo

February 25, 1990

In the early morning, a loud thud awakens Michael Schiavo in his St. Petersburg, Florida, apartment. Scrambling out of bed, Michael discovers his twenty-six-year-old wife, Terri, by the doorway separating the bathroom from the hallway, lying face down on the floor. She isn't moving. He tries speaking to her, but she doesn't answer. He calls 911. Within minutes, the paramedics arrive. Terri, they quickly determine, is in cardiac arrest. They are able to get her heart beating again and rush her, still unconscious, to nearby Humana Northside Hospital.

The doctors treat Terri for an apparent heart attack. A blood assay reveals that she has a potassium imbalance, which the doctors suspect triggered the heart attack. Her low level of potassium, some doctors later suggest, was the result of bulimia. As a child Terri was obese – at one point, standing at 5' 3", she weighed 200 pounds – but while she was a teenager she lost 65 pounds. After that she struggled to keep her weight under control. At the time of her collapse, she was dieting, drinking ten to fifteen glasses of iced tea a day. She weighed 120 pounds.

Despite the doctors' best efforts, Terri doesn't regain consciousness.

The days and weeks following

Terri's neurologists conduct a series of tests. Does she respond to simple commands, such as "Squeeze my hand"? No. Do her eyes track moving objects? No. Do her pupils respond to light? No. Does she show signs that she recognizes her husband or her parents? No. Terri shows no signs of cognitive functioning.

CT scans reveal that Terri's cerebral cortex is severely damaged, the damage caused by a lack of oxygen to the brain during Terri's cardiac arrest. Terri's brain stem, however, is functioning. Because her brain stem is functional, Terri is able to breathe, she is able to blink, her heart is able to beat, and her body is able to go through the regular cycles of sleeping and waking.

Eventually the doctors reach a diagnosis: Terri is in a persistent vegetative state (PVS). PVS differs from both brain death and a minimally conscious state. Brain dead patients show no brain activity at all, not even in the brain stem. Without the aid of machinery, such patients are unable to breathe, and their hearts are unable to beat. PVS patients, by contrast, have a functioning brain stem. They don't, however, have any awareness of themselves or of the world around them. This makes PVS patients different from minimally conscious patients, who have at least some awareness at least some of the time.

Sometimes a PVS patient improves, but, if improvement occurs, it usually does so within the first three months. After six months, PVS patients almost never regain even minimal consciousness, but remain vegetative for the rest of their lives. Such patients can't eat or drink on their own; they must be fed through a gastric tube surgically implanted in their stomachs, and they must be hydrated through an IV line. Because they easily get infections, they must be given IV antibiotics prophylactically. They must also lie on special mattresses and be periodically moved to prevent bedsores. Some PVS patients live like this for decades.

This is the future that Terri faces.

June 18, 1990

Michael is appointed Terri's guardian. Terri's parents, Robert and Mary Schindler, don't object. The Schindlers get along well with Michael. In fact, Michael is now living with the Schindlers in the Schindlers' home, also in St. Petersburg, Florida.

June 1990 to February 1993

Michael aggressively pursues a variety of treatments for his wife. For example, in November 1990 he takes Terri to California for experimental "brain stimulator" treatment, and in July 1991 he transfers Terri to Sable Palms, a skilled care facility in Florida, where she receives ongoing neurological testing and speech/occupational therapy. If he doesn't like something her care providers are doing, he doesn't hesitate to express his concerns. Despite all that he does for her, however, Terri's condition shows no improvement.

In November 1992 Michael sues the gynecologists Terri had before she collapsed. His argument is that the gynecologists failed to detect the potassium imbalance that resulted in Terri's heart attack, which in turn led to Terri's brain damage. Michael wins the lawsuit. He is awarded $750,000 for Terri's ongoing care and an additional $300,000 for his loss and suffering.

1993

In February Michael has a falling out with the Schindlers. The Schindlers claim they are concerned about the course of therapy that Michael is providing for their daughter. In July the Schindlers sue Michael, asking the court that they be allowed to replace Michael as Terri's legal guardians. The lawsuit is eventually dismissed. Michael claims that the dispute is really over the $300,000 that he was awarded the previous year, that the Schindlers are trying to force him to share the money with them.

1994

Michael asks his wife's doctors how likely it is that she'll ever regain consciousness. When the doctors tell him that this is extremely unlikely, Michael asks that his wife not be resuscitated if she suffers a heart attack or if some other life-threatening event occurs. Michael also begins a relationship with Jodi Centonze, and later has two children with her. Michael's relationship with the Schindlers continues to deteriorate.

1998 to 2000

In May 1998 Michael petitions the Circuit Court for Pinellas County in Florida to allow him to remove the gastric tube that feeds Terri so that she can die. He admits that Terri left no written instructions, but he claims that on several occasions she told him that she would not want to live in a vegetative state with no chance of recovery. A handful of Terri's acquaintances make similar claims, but the Schindlers disagree. They argue that they raised their daughter as a Roman Catholic, that Roman Catholicism opposes ending the lives of PVS patients, and that consequently their daughter would not want her feeding tube removed.

On December 29, 1999, Richard Pearse, the court-appointed guardian ad litem – or person advocating for the best interests of Terri – issues his report. In his report Pearse expresses his suspicion that, by seeking to remove his wife's feeding tube, Michael may be thinking more about his own interests than those of his wife. The basis of the suspicion is that, if his wife were to die, he, as the husband, would inherit the entirety of her estate. Pearse suggests that this might explain why Michael has opted not to divorce his wife and marry Ms. Centonze – if he were to do that, the Schindlers would be the ones to inherit Terri's estate.

Despite Pearse's suspicions, on February 11, 2000, George Greer, the presiding judge for the Circuit Court for Pinellas County, rules that Michael may remove his wife's feeding tube. Greer argues that Michael's motivations are irrelevant, that the only relevant issues at hand are 1) whether Terri has any chance of improving and 2) what Terri would want. According to Terri's doctors, the answer to the first question is "No," and, as for the second question, Judge Greer sees sufficient evidence that Terri would not want to live the rest of her life in a vegetative state. The Schindlers, who, contrary to what the medical experts claim, believe that their daughter has a chance of regaining consciousness, appeal Judge Greer's decision.

April 2001

On April 24, after all appeals have been exhausted and the U.S. Supreme Court has declined to review the case, Terri's feeding tube is removed. Two days later the Schindlers sue Michael on the grounds that he committed perjury when he stated that his wife wouldn't want to live in a vegetative state with no chance of recovery. The courts order that Terri's feeding tube be reinserted until this new lawsuit comes to a conclusion.

2001 to 2003

The Schindlers continue their legal maneuvers to block the removal of their daughter's feeding tube, and they enlist the support of prolife groups and conservative Christians. In violation of a court order, they release a videotape of Terri that convinces many viewers that she has some cognitive abilities. They repeatedly accuse Michael of abuse, claiming that he is neglecting Terri's hygiene, denying her dental care, poisoning her, and physically harming her. The Florida Department of Children and Families investigates all the charges but finds no evidence of abuse. The Schindlers also claim that Terri never had a heart attack, but instead that Michael strangled her but failed to kill her, and that's how she ended up in a vegetative state. All of these maneuvers, however, ultimately fail.

October 2003

On October 15, Terri's feeding tube is removed for the second time. In response the Florida state legislature passes "Terri's Law," allowing Governor Jeb Bush, brother of President George W. Bush, to order that the feeding tube be replaced. Governor Bush issues the order on October 21.

2004

In September the Florida Supreme Court rules that "Terri's Law" is unconstitutional. The reason the law is unconstitutional is that it violates the separation of powers – that is, by passing "Terri's Law," the Florida legislature attempted to do what only the courts are allowed to do. In October Governor Bush says he will file a petition with the U.S. Supreme Court.

January 2005

The U.S. Supreme Court refuses to review the case.

March 18, 2005

For the third time Terri's feeding tube is removed.

March 21, 2005

The U.S. Senate and House of Representatives pass the Palm Sunday Compromise, and President George W. Bush signs it. The Palm Sunday Compromise is an attempt to save Terri's life by allowing the federal courts to hear the case: "The United States District Court for the Middle District of Florida shall have jurisdiction to hear, determine, and render judgment on a suit or claim by or on behalf of Theresa Marie Schiavo for the alleged violation of any right of Theresa Marie Schiavo under the Constitution or laws of the United States relating to the withholding or withdrawal of food, fluids, or medical treatment necessary to sustain her life."

March 22, 2005

The United States District Court for the Middle District of Florida refuses to order the reinsertion of Terri's feeding tube.

March 31, 2005

Protesters stand outside Woodside Hospice, where Terri is a patient. Many of them carry signs. The messages on the signs convey anger:

"Murder Is Legal in America," "Hospice or Auschwitz," "Hey, Judge, Who Made You God?" Inside the hospice, cradling Terri's head, is Michael. Shortly after 9:00 a.m., Terri stops breathing – she dies as a result of dehydration. The Schindlers are not present – at Michael's request.

April 1, 2005
Terri's body is cremated, after an extensive autopsy has been conducted.

June 15, 2005
The results of the autopsy are made public. The original diagnosis of PVS was correct. Because of the lack of oxygen caused by the cardiac arrest, Terri's brain shrank to less than half its normal weight. Terri would never have regained even minimal cognitive functioning, no matter what treatment the doctors prescribed.

The autopsy reveals no signs of strangulation or abuse. It also reveals no evidence of a heart attack. According to the report, Terri had a potassium imbalance, but the imbalance was discovered only after the doctors at the hospital had given her several drugs known to lower potassium in the blood. This casts doubt on the claim that a potassium imbalance caused Terri's cardiac arrest, as well as on the claim that Terri suffered from bulimia. As the autopsy report states, "No one observed [Terri] taking diet pills, binging and purging or consuming laxatives, and she apparently never confessed to her family or friends about having an eating disorder."

What, then, caused Terri's cardiac arrest? No one knows. The autopsy report concludes, "The manner of death will therefore be certified as undetermined."

January 2006
Michael marries Jodi Centonze. The couple and their two children continue to live in Florida.

Should Michael have sought to remove Terri's feeding tube? Should the Schindlers have tried to block Michael's efforts? Did the courts make appropriate rulings? Should Terri have been allowed to die?

Part 2
PARENTS AND CHILDREN

Case Study 9
Miss Sherri

Sherri Finkbine of Phoenix, Arizona, is best known for two things. First, in the early 1960s she hosted the Phoenix version of the popular children's television program *Romper Room*. The purpose of the show was to teach kindergarten-age children how to be polite and well-behaved. The children who appeared on the show addressed Finkbine as Miss Sherri (even though Finkbine was married), and Miss Sherri introduced the children to Mr. Do-Bee (a man in a bumblebee suit who embodied how children *should* behave) and Mr. Don't-Bee (a man in a bumblebee suit who exemplified how children *shouldn't* behave). The second thing Finkbine is known for is the abortion she had in 1962.

Finkbine had already had four children and was in the early stages of her fifth pregnancy. The pregnancy was normal enough, except that Finkbine suffered from insomnia. Her husband had recently returned from a trip to Europe and had brought back with him some pills that were easily available there. Many pregnant women in Europe were taking the pills – the pills eased the symptoms of morning sickness, and they helped with insomnia. Finkbine started taking the pills too.

A few weeks later, Finkbine learned that large numbers of European women were giving birth to seriously impaired children. Some of the children had no arms or legs, or their hands grew directly out of their shoulders. Others suffered from defects in the eyes, ears, or internal organs. Many of the children didn't survive. The cause of the deformities, Finkbine learned, was thalidomide, a drug that many pregnant women in Europe were taking. Finkbine wondered if the pills she was taking contained thalidomide. She decided to see her doctor. By then, she had already taken thirty-six of the pills.

Finkbine's doctor delivered the bad news. Yes, the pills contained thalidomide and yes, the probability that Finkbine would give birth to a seriously impaired child was high. The doctor recommended an abortion; Finkbine agreed. In 1962, abortion was illegal in Arizona, except when the woman needed an abortion to save her life. Finkbine's doctor believed that, although Finkbine's life wasn't likely at stake, the three-member medical board of Phoenix would probably grant her an abortion, since she had good medical reasons. When she requested an abortion, the medical board granted it.

Finkbine believed she had a duty to share her story, so that other pregnant women would know not to take thalidomide. She contacted a local newspaper. The editor agreed to tell her story without using her name. The headline read "Baby-Deforming Drug May Cost Woman Her Child Here." When the story was published, Finkbine was still pregnant; she hadn't yet gotten her abortion.

Soon the story went national, and Finkbine's identity was revealed. Finkbine found herself the target of antiabortion sentiments. One writer said, "I hope someone takes the other four children and strangles them, because it is all the same thing." Another, writing from the perspective of Finkbine's fetus, said, "Mommy, please dear Mommy, let me live. Please, please, I want to live. Let me love you, let me see the light of day, let me smell a rose, let me sing a song, let me look into your face, let me say Mommy." The official Vatican newspaper, *Il Osservatore Romano*, accused Finkbine and her husband of murder.

In the face of the public outcry, Finkbine lost her job hosting *Romper Room*. In addition, the medical board of Phoenix reversed its decision. Finkbine wouldn't be able to get an abortion after all, at least not in Arizona. Finkbine tried other states where the abortion laws were less restrictive, but she couldn't find a doctor who was willing to help her. In the end, she flew to Sweden and got her abortion there. The Swedish obstetrician informed her that the fetus had no legs and only one arm, and wouldn't have survived.

Finkbine's story raises several moral questions. Is abortion morally permissible when the fetus is seriously impaired? How serious must the impairment be before an abortion is justified? Suppose a woman discovers that, if she gives birth, her child will be blind or deaf. Would aborting such a child be morally acceptable? What if the child would be born with Down syndrome, and therefore be mentally retarded? What if the child would be born with the Huntington's gene, living the first forty or so years of her or his life in good health and only then becoming sick and dying after another fifteen or twenty years? What if the child would be born with Tay-Sachs disease, a lipid metabolism disorder that causes death in the first one to four years of life?

As opponents of abortion often point out, even those with serious illnesses or disabilities usually say they were glad they were born. This suggests, according to opponents of abortion, that life is a precious gift

– indeed, the most precious gift of all, since it's a prerequisite for all other gifts one might enjoy. What makes abortion wrong, opponents of abortion conclude, is that it denies the fetus of this most precious of gifts.

Some defenders of abortion counter this reasoning with an argument known as the replaceability argument. Suppose a woman who has four children, as Finkbine did, plans to have one, and only one, more child. She becomes pregnant with a fifth child and then discovers, again as Finkbine did, that her fetus has a serious impairment. Now she faces a choice. On the one hand, if she continues with her pregnancy, she'll give her fetus the precious gift of life, but she won't give the precious gift of life to any more children. On the other hand, if she terminates her pregnancy, she'll deny her fetus the precious gift of life, but she'll go on to have another child, granting this next child the precious gift of life. In effect, she'll replace one child with another. Furthermore, in most cases when a woman aborts an impaired child, her next child is healthier. Surely, according to the replaceability argument, it's better to bring a healthy child into the world than an impaired child. Surely, in a case like this, it's best to abort the impaired child.

But is a fetus, seriously impaired or otherwise, replaceable? Some things, such as pens, seem clearly replaceable – when one pen runs out of ink, we replace it with another, and we don't think we've done anything wrong. Other things, such as our teenaged children, seem clearly irreplaceable – even if they should lose two legs and an arm, like Finkbine's fetus, we shouldn't kill them and then conceive another, healthier child. According to the replaceability argument, what makes our teenaged children irreplaceable is that they have a sense of their own future. They may, for example, have plans to go to college, start their own business, and get married. If we kill them, they would lose this future that they're looking forward to. This is why killing them for the purpose of conceiving another, healthier child is wrong. Fetuses, however, like pens, have no sense of their future. They don't look forward to going to college, starting their own business, or getting married. If we kill a fetus, it doesn't lose anything that it values. As such, it is replaceable.

Or so the replaceability argument says. Is the replaceability argument convincing?

Case Study 10
Roe v. Wade

The Plaintiff

Norma McCorvey had a tough childhood. Her father left the family when she was thirteen, and her mother was a violent alcoholic. At age fourteen, after having been raped at a reform school, McCorvey dropped out of school. Two years later, she got married, but then separated from her husband when he started beating her. By the time she was twenty-one, she had already given birth to two children, each having a different father, and she was pregnant with a third child.

The first child was raised by McCorvey's mother, the second by the child's father. McCorvey didn't want to have a third child; she wanted to get an abortion. But it was 1969, and she was living in Texas. At that time, abortion was illegal in Texas, except in cases of rape or incest, or when a woman needed an abortion to save her life. McCorvey claimed – falsely – that she had been raped, but her scheme fell apart when she was unable to produce evidence of rape. She considered traveling to California, where the law was less restrictive, and getting an abortion there, but she didn't have enough money for that. Finally, she attempted to visit an illegal abortion clinic in Dallas, but that didn't work either, because authorities had already shut the clinic down. McCorvey appeared to be out of options.

That was when two lawyers – Linda Coffee and Sarah Weddington – approached her. Coffee and Weddington hoped to file a class-action lawsuit that would challenge the constitutionality of the Texas abortion law. To file the lawsuit, they needed a plaintiff. They asked McCorvey if she'd be willing to be the plaintiff. The only condition was that McCorvey not get an abortion before the case was decided – if she did, the court might rule that the case was moot and thus do nothing to change the law. McCorvey agreed to the terms.

Unfortunately for McCorvey, the case dragged on – she gave birth to a girl, which she gave up for adoption. Eventually, in December 1971, when the girl was two years old, the case came before the United States Supreme Court. The case was *Roe v. Wade*. McCorvey, assigned the name Jane Roe to protect her privacy, found herself involved in what would be one of the most famous court cases of all time.

The Decision

The Supreme Court handed down its landmark 7-2 decision on January 23, 1973. Ruling against the Texas law, the majority of the justices declared that women have a constitutional right to get an abortion. Before *Roe*, it was up to each state whether or not to allow abortions. Some states did, but most, like Texas, didn't – except in extreme circumstances such as rape. After *Roe*, however, all states had to allow abortions – though states could still place certain restrictions on abortion.

To reach its decision, the Court addressed three questions:

1) Does a woman seeking an abortion have a right to privacy? A right to privacy is a right to do something without interference from the state. In the United States people's right to privacy is extensive, but it's also limited. Thus, I may get drunk, but I may not drink and drive. I may smoke, but I may not puff smoke in other people's faces. I may view pornographic materials, but I may not view child pornography. What, then, about a woman who wishes to terminate her pregnancy? Should she be allowed to do so without interference from the state? The Supreme Court admitted that, just as the state has a legitimate interest in protecting people from drunk drivers and secondhand smoke and pedophiles, so it has a legitimate interest in protecting fetuses. It has this interest because fetuses represent the future of society and the state has a legitimate interest in the future of society. But does the state's interest in protecting fetuses carry greater weight than a woman's desire to terminate her pregnancy, or does a woman's desire to terminate her pregnancy carry greater weight than the state's interest in protecting fetuses? According to the Court, the answer depends on whether the fetus is viable. A fetus is said to be viable if it can be removed from the womb and still survive, either with or without the aid of machinery, such as respirators. The Court determined, then, that a woman seeking an abortion has a right to privacy, but only before her fetus is viable. Once the fetus becomes viable, the state's interest in protecting the fetus takes precedence. (In 1973 a fetus became viable around twenty-six weeks after conception, or at the beginning of the third trimester of pregnancy. Today, thanks to improved technology, the point at which fetuses become viable occurs earlier in pregnancy – some fetuses are viable as early as twenty

weeks after conception, and most are viable twenty-four weeks after conception.)

2) Is abortion a medically safe procedure for the woman? To answer the second question, the justices of the Supreme Court turned to the considered judgments of physicians. Physicians reported that, during the first trimester of pregnancy, abortion is reasonably safe, but is only sometimes safe thereafter. The Court accepted this view. (Today abortion is somewhat safer than it was in 1973: less than 1% of women who have abortions experience major complications, and the probability of a woman dying from an abortion is eleven times lower than the probability of a woman dying from childbirth, although the exact risk of death associated with abortion increases as the pregnancy continues. If an abortion is performed within the first eight weeks of pregnancy, the risk of death is one in a million; if it is performed more than twenty weeks after conception, the risk of death is one in 11,000.)

3) Is a fetus a person? According to the Court, this question is the most important of the three. For suppose it turns out that a fetus is a person. Since the Constitution accords all persons a right to life, a fetus would have a right to life, and, since an abortion would kill the fetus, an abortion would violate the fetus' right to life. Thus, if a fetus is a person, the Court would have had to rule against abortion rights – no matter how the Court answered the first two questions. But is a fetus a person? The Court noted that the experts on this question – doctors, theologians, and philosophers – were divided. Some insisted that a fetus is a person, while others were equally convinced that a fetus isn't a person. Since the experts had yet to reach a consensus, the Court concluded that, at least for the time being, the answer to the third question is unknown. The Court therefore felt compelled to base its decision solely on the answers it gave to the first two questions. (The question whether a fetus is a person continues to be controversial in the twenty-first century. Doctors, theologians, and philosophers are no closer to reaching a consensus.)

The Court summed up its decision as follows. A woman has an absolute right to get an abortion during the first trimester of her pregnancy. After the first trimester but before the fetus is viable, the only grounds the state can have for preventing an abortion is if the attending physicians determine that an abortion would put the woman's life or health at risk. Once the fetus is viable, though, the state may refuse to allow an abortion.

McCorvey's Conversion

For a decade after *Roe v. Wade*, Norma McCorvey remained anonymous – and poor. Without even a high school education, she could get only low-paying jobs such as waitressing and bartending. In the 1980s she revealed to the public that she was Jane Roe. She received a flurry of attention and got a job at a women's clinic. In 1994, with the help of a coauthor, she wrote about her life in *I Am Roe*.

Then came an astonishing turn of events. Operation Rescue, an antiabortion organization, set up an office in Dallas, next to the women's clinic where McCorvey worked. McCorvey was initially unsympathetic to Operation Rescue's activities, but eventually, while taking cigarette breaks, she befriended Philip Benham, a preacher who worked with Operation Rescue. Benham persuaded her to attend church, and she soon converted to Roman Catholicism. On August 8, 1995, in a backyard pool in Dallas, she was baptized. Shortly after, she publicly announced that she was now opposed to abortion.

In 1998, with the help of another coauthor, McCorvey wrote a second book, *Won by Love*. In this book, she explained what led her to become an antiabortionist:

> I was sitting in O.R.'s [Operation Rescue's] offices when I noticed a fetal development poster. The progression was so obvious, the eyes were so sweet. It hurt my heart, just looking at them. I ran outside and finally, it dawned on me. "Norma," I said to myself, "they're right." I had worked with pregnant women for years. I had been through three pregnancies and deliveries myself. I should have known. Yet something in that poster made me lose my breath. I kept seeing the picture of that tiny, 10-week-old embryo, and I said to myself, that's a baby! It's as if blinders just fell off my eyes and I suddenly understood the truth – that's a baby!

In this passage, McCorvey claimed to know what the justices of the Supreme Court claimed not to know – that a fetus, even as young as ten weeks after conception, is a baby, a person. Was McCorvey right? What is a person? Is a fetus a person? If a fetus is a person, does it follow that abortion is wrong? Did the Supreme Court reach the right decision in *Roe v. Wade*, or was its decision a mistake?

Case Study 11
The Octomom

On January 26, 2009, in Bellflower, California, thirty-three-year-old Nadya Suleman, who now goes by the name of Natalie, gave birth to octuplets. The eight babies – six boys and two girls – beat the heaviest of odds. A woman carrying just half that many babies has a twenty-five percent chance of miscarrying in the first trimester, while a woman carrying five babies has a fifty percent chance. Suleman gave birth by Caesarian section after just thirty-one weeks of pregnancy – rather than the normal forty weeks – and so her eight babies were fragile and small, the smallest weighing a mere one pound, eight ounces. All of the babies, though, were born in stable condition, and, thanks to expert medical care, all of them are still alive and healthy ten years later. Suleman's babies were only the second set of octuplets to be born in the United States, and they're the only set of octuplets all of whom survived more than a week.

The public's initial reaction to the eight births was one of awe. People assumed that Suleman, like other women who give birth to high order multiples, had had difficulties becoming pregnant, that, desperate to have a child, she sought out the services of a fertility specialist, and that now, instead of having just one child, her hands were full with eight. Working under these assumptions, people sympathized with Suleman, and wished her and the babies well.

This initial reaction, however, didn't last long. As soon as the babies were born, the media began intensively scrutinizing Suleman, and quickly uncovered a number of facts.

First, Suleman already had six other children – four boys and two girls, the first child born in 2001. Like the octuplets, the six earlier children were born with the help of a fertility specialist. According to Suleman's mother, the father of all fourteen children was David Solomon, a friend of Suleman. In February 2009, another man, Denis Beaudoin, who claimed to have dated Suleman from 1997 to 1999, said that he, not Solomon, was the father. Suleman's ex-husband, Marcos Gutierrez, denied fathering any of the children.

Second, Suleman was divorced. She had married Gutierrez in 1996, but the two separated in 2000. In 2006 Gutierrez filed for divorce, which was finalized in 2008. According to Gutierrez, the marriage ended because the couple had difficulty having children. Suleman wanted to try in vitro fertilization, but Gutierrez was opposed.

Third, Suleman was unemployed. For a time she had worked at Metropolitan State Hospital as a psychiatric technician. In 1999 she claimed that she hurt her back in the performance of her duties there and was eventually awarded $167,000 in worker's compensation benefits. Presumably it was this money that Suleman used to pay for the in vitro fertilization treatments (each of which cost between $12,000 and $15,000) that helped her conceive her fourteen children. Suleman then went back to school, earning her bachelor's degree in child and adolescent development in 2006 from California State University, Fullerton. She enrolled in a master's program in counseling, also at CSUF, but dropped out in 2008. At the time she gave birth to the octuplets, her sole source of income was from public welfare programs. Thus, Suleman had no way to pay the $1.3 million hospital costs for the birth and care of her octuplets, and she had no way to support her fourteen children. These costs would have to be borne by the public.

When these facts came to light, the initially sympathetic public turned hostile. Some accused Suleman of taking advantage of the welfare system, having large numbers of children so she'd never have to work again. Others believed that Suleman was psychologically unstable, with a compulsion to have children. Suleman had death threats issued against her, and on April 1, 2009, vandals threw a baby seat through the rear window of her Toyota minivan. Picking up on the hostility, the tabloid media nicknamed Suleman "the Octomom." Suleman responded to the criticisms leveled against her. She claimed that she loved children and that she planned to return to school, get her master's degree in counseling, and find a job to support her family. Suleman's statements did little to assuage the public's resentment.

Although most of the public's anger was directed at Suleman, some people were also angry with Suleman's fertility specialist, Dr. Michael Kamrava. According to Suleman, Dr. Kamrava transferred six embryos to her uterus, all that were left over after giving birth to her first six children. When two of the six embryos split into twins, Suleman carried octuplets. Dr. Kamrava, however, later acknowledged that the number of embryos he transferred to Suleman's uterus was twelve rather than six. Although no law prohibited the transfer of so many embryos, Dr. Kamrava violated the guidelines of the American Society for Reproductive Medicine, according to which, for a woman Suleman's age (under thirty-five), the number of embryos transferred should not exceed two. The reason for limiting the number of transfers is to avoid the risks associated with high order multiple pregnancies – for example, miscarriage and premature births.

But why did Dr. Kamrava agree to transfer any embryos at all, knowing that Suleman was single, unemployed, and already a mother of six children? Shouldn't he have realized that Suleman wouldn't be able to support an even larger family, that the welfare system – that is, taxpayers – would have to foot the bill? Many argued that Dr. Kamrava was just as irresponsible as Suleman.

Finally, given that Dr. Kamrava transferred twelve embryos and that Suleman became pregnant with a large number of fetuses, why didn't Dr. Kamrava insist on selective reduction – that is, the elimination of some of the fetuses in order to improve the odds of the other fetuses, as well as to minimize the risks for Suleman? In cases of high order multiple pregnancies, selective reduction is a standard procedure. Sometimes, though, women with high order multiple pregnancies reject selective reduction, because they oppose abortion. This is what Mary Atwood, pregnant with eight fetuses, did in England. She agreed to sell her story to a tabloid, with the amount of money she received depending on how many of the eight babies survived. She had a miscarriage and lost all eight.

Was the public's hostility to Suleman an overreaction? Was Suleman irresponsible? Was Dr. Kamrava irresponsible? How many embryos should Dr. Kamrava have transferred to Suleman's uterus? What, precisely, should be the responsibilities of fertility specialists? Should they be responsible only for helping clients become pregnant and give birth? Or should they also be responsible for determining whether a client will be a fit parent, and whether the client will be able to support her children rather than having taxpayers pay the costs?

Postscript: For violating the guidelines of the American Society for Reproductive Medicine, Dr. Kamrava had his license revoked by the Medical Board of California on July 1, 2011. In the years since she gave birth to the octuplets, Natalie Suleman has done little to rehabilitate her reputation. In the summer of 2012, she appeared in an adult film, and she started working in men's clubs dancing as an adult entertainer. In October 2012 she checked herself into Chapman House Treatment

Center in Los Angeles, for a month of treatment for anxiety, exhaustion, and stress. She had been taking Xanax for her problems. In July 2014 she pleaded no contest to charges of welfare fraud – she had failed to disclose that she'd earned nearly $30,000 from videos and interviews at the same time she was receiving welfare benefits. She was sentenced to 200 hours of community service and two years of probation.

Case Study 12
Baby M

William Stern, a biochemist living in Tenafly, New Jersey, wanted to have children. His desire was, as he put it, "compelling," because he didn't have relatives "anywhere in the world," all of them having been killed by the Nazis. He and his wife, Elizabeth, planned to start a family after she finished her medical residency in 1981, but in 1979 Mrs. Stern was diagnosed with optic neuritis, an eye condition that suggested she had multiple sclerosis. When a medical colleague told her that pregnancy might, given her condition, cause her to become temporarily or permanently paralyzed, the Sterns rethought their plans. "We decided the risk wasn't worth it," Mr. Stern said.

The Sterns sought help from the Infertility Center of New York, where, in January of 1985, they met Mary Beth Whitehead and her husband, Richard. Mrs. Whitehead was not a client of the infertility center – she was fertile, with two children, a son and a daughter. But she understood what infertile couples go through, because her sister was infertile. This was what drew her to the infertility center – she hoped to help infertile couples. So when she learned of the Sterns' difficulties, Mrs. Whitehead agreed to become a surrogate mother on their behalf. The Sterns were delighted; they believed that Mrs. Whitehead was a "perfect person" to help them.

A surrogate mother is a woman (such as Mrs. Whitehead) who bears a child on behalf of another woman (such as Mrs. Stern). Sometimes the surrogate not only bears the child but is also the biological mother – the child is the union of her egg with the sperm of the other woman's partner. At other times the surrogate isn't the biological mother – she is artificially inseminated with the fertilized egg of the other woman. While the latter kind of surrogate is called a *gestational surrogate*, the former is called a *genetic surrogate*. Mrs. Whitehead would be a genetic surrogate.

Thus, Mrs. Whitehead agreed to be artificially inseminated with her own egg fertilized by Mr. Stern's sperm, and then, when she gave birth, she would hand the child over to the Sterns. As the surrogacy contract she signed stated, "Mary Beth Whitehead understands and agrees that in the best interest of the child, she will not form or attempt to form a parent-child relationship with any child or children she may conceive, carry to term and give birth to, pursuant to the provisions of this Agreement, and shall freely surrender custody to William Stern, Natural Father, immediately upon birth of the child; and terminate all parental rights to said child." In return, Mr. Stern agreed to pay Mrs. Whitehead $10,000 upon receiving the child, plus whatever medical expenses Mrs. Whitehead incurred as a result of her pregnancy. He also agreed to pay $7,500 to the Infertility Center of New York, for arranging the deal.

On March 27, 1986, Mrs. Whitehead gave birth to a baby girl, whom she named Sara. Three days later, on March 30, she turned the baby over to the Sterns. The Sterns named the girl Melissa.

A few hours after turning the baby over, Mrs. Whitehead called the Sterns. She was distraught. "She said she didn't know if she could live anymore," said Mrs. Stern. The next morning she called again, asking the Sterns if she could see the baby. Before noon she and her sister were at the Sterns' house. According to Mrs. Stern, Mrs. Whitehead said that her husband was threatening to leave her, that she "woke up screaming in the middle of the night" because she no longer had the baby, and that she had "considered taking a bottle of valium." She asked the Sterns if they would let her have the baby for a week, promising them that thereafter "I'll be out of your lives forever." Concerned that Mrs. Whitehead might commit suicide if they said no, the Sterns granted the request.

A week later Mrs. Whitehead informed the Sterns that she intended to keep the baby. In response, the Sterns got a court order and went to the Whiteheads' home, where, accompanied by five police officers, they demanded the return of their child. Mrs. Whitehead, however, slipped the baby out of a window to her husband, and the next morning she and her husband fled to Florida with the baby. For the next three months, the Whiteheads evaded police by staying in some twenty different hotels, motels, and homes. From time to time, Mrs. Whitehead called Mr. Stern, threatening to kill herself and the child, and threatening falsely to accuse Mr. Stern of molesting her older daughter. Finally, near the end of July 1986, while Mrs. Whitehead was in the hospital with a kidney infection, the police raided her mother's home in Florida, where the baby was being kept, and took the baby back to the Sterns in New Jersey.

The Whiteheads returned to New Jersey, where they filed a lawsuit in an attempt to regain custody of the girl they knew as Sara. The case became known as the Baby M case.

On March 31, 1987, just over a year after the baby was born, Judge Harvey R. Sorkow handed down his decision. Ruling in favor of the Sterns, he argued that the surrogacy contract was valid. A deal was a deal, he thought, and changing one's mind isn't enough to nullify a deal.

According to Sorkow, Mrs. Whitehead's consent to the terms of the contract was fully free and informed: "Neither party has a superior bargaining position. Each had what the other wanted. A price for the service each was to perform was struck and a bargain reached. One did not force the other. Neither had expertise that left the other at a disadvantage. Neither had disproportionate bargaining power."

Sorkow also rejected the contention that the contract involved the selling of a baby – in essence, that Mr. Stern was paying $10,000 for a child. If this had been the case, the contract would have been invalid, because selling and buying people is illegal and immoral – it treats people as mere means. In Sorkow's view, however, the $10,000 was for Mrs. Whitehead's nine months of service rather than for the baby: "At birth, the father does not purchase the child. It is his own biological genetically related child. He cannot purchase what is already his."

Finally, Sorkow argued that paid pregnancy is similar to paid sperm donation. If we allow the one, then, to be consistent, we must allow the other: "If a man may offer the means for procreation then a woman must equally be allowed to do so." Not allowing women to do so would, according to Sorkow, deny them the equal protection of the law.

The Whiteheads appealed Sorkow's decision. Nearly a year later, on February 3, 1988, in a unanimous ruling, the New Jersey Supreme Court reversed Sorkow's decision, finding surrogacy contracts to be invalid. Writing for the court was Chief Justice Robert Wilentz.

First, unlike Sorkow, Wilentz held that a paid surrogate's consent is neither completely voluntary nor fully informed. She is compelled by "the inducement of a $10,000 payment," and, under the contract, "the natural mother is irrevocably committed before she knows the strength of her bond with her child. She never makes a totally voluntary, informed decision, for quite clearly any decision prior to the baby's birth is, in the most important sense, uninformed." But was Mrs. Whitehead's decision to become a surrogate mother really uninformed?

Given that she'd already had two children and must have experienced the powerful bond that mothers normally form with their babies, shouldn't she have known that her bond with the third child – Baby M – would likely be just as strong? According to Wilentz, no, she couldn't have known that, because she went into her third pregnancy with a different mindset than she did with her first two pregnancies, expressly intending to give the child up. Because she intended to give the child up, she may have thought that she wouldn't form such a strong bond with her.

Second, also unlike Sorkow, Wilentz argued that the $10,000 payment was not for Whitehead's nine months of service, but for the baby, since, under the contract, Mrs. Whitehead could collect the $10,000 only after giving up the child and surrendering her parental rights. Thus, paid surrogacy, according to Wilentz, amounts to baby-selling: "This is the sale of a child, or, at the very least, the sale of a mother's right to her child, the only mitigating factor being that one of the purchasers is the father." Wilentz concluded, "There are, in a civilized society, some things that money cannot buy."

Having found the surrogacy contract invalid, the New Jersey Supreme Court handed the case back to a lower court to determine who should get custody of Baby M. The lower court ruled that custody should go to the Sterns, since they could provide a more stable home environment for the child than could the Whiteheads. However, since Mrs. Whitehead was the biological mother of the child, the lower court granted her visitation rights.

Did the New Jersey Supreme Court reach the right decision, or was Sorkow's decision better? Should surrogacy contracts be upheld? Should the Sterns have received custody of Baby M? Should Mrs. Whitehead have been granted visitation rights?

Postscript: To this day, paid surrogacy remains illegal in New Jersey. In some other states it is also illegal, but in some states it is legal and some states have no clearly established law one way or the other. When Melissa Stern turned eighteen, she cut off contact with Mary Beth Whitehead and was legally adopted by Elizabeth Stern. Mary Beth and Richard Whitehead are no longer married.

Case Study 13
Savior Sibling

One day in 1988, sixteen-year-old Anissa Ayala discovered lumps on her ankles. Not long after, she developed severe pains in her stomach. When her parents, Abe and Mary Ayala, took her to the hospital, the diagnosis was worse than they could ever have imagined – Anissa had a rare form of leukemia. She underwent radiation and chemotherapy treatments, which successfully destroyed her diseased bone marrow and blood cells. However, as a result of her treatments, Anissa's bone marrow could no longer produce sufficient quantities of normal blood cells. Without a bone marrow transplant, Anissa would almost certainly die.

Unfortunately, neither her older brother, Airon, nor her parents were suitable donors. The Ayalas tried their luck with a public bone-marrow registry, but this didn't work either. The chances of finding a compatible donor among non-relatives are one in 20,000, and the only compatible donor the Ayalas found backed out. The Ayalas seemed to be out of options.

Then Abe and Mary had an idea. Perhaps they could have another child, and perhaps the new child would be a suitable donor. The plan was a long shot. First, Abe would have to have his vasectomy successfully reversed. Second, Mary, who was now forty-two years old, well past her most fertile years, would have to become pregnant and give birth. Third, the child would have to be a compatible donor – only a one in four probability. Fourth, Anissa's health would have to hold up until the child was old enough for a bone marrow transplant. Finally, the bone marrow transplant would have to be successful. The likelihood that all of these things would happen was remote to say the least. Anissa's physician discouraged Abe and Mary from carrying out their plan. Abe and Mary, however, were desperate – despite the physician's advice, Abe underwent surgery to reverse his vasectomy.

The surgery worked, and soon Mary was pregnant. In February of 1990, tests performed on the fetus revealed that it would make an ideal donor for Anissa. The baby was born on April 6 – a healthy six-pound girl. Abe and Mary named the girl Marissa. Fourteen months later,

Marissa was old enough to donate her marrow. She was placed under general anesthesia, and marrow was taken from her hip and then injected into Anissa's veins. The procedure went well. Soon Anissa's bone marrow started to produce normal blood cells. Against all odds, Marissa had saved Anissa's life – she was a savior sibling.

In its June 17, 1991, issue, *Time* magazine reported the story. Some readers were happy for the Ayalas, but many responded with harsh criticism. Abe and Mary, the critics charged, used Marissa as a mere means, bringing her into existence not for her sake but for Anissa's sake. Marissa had never consented to be a savior sibling. She didn't agree to undergo general anesthesia, to have a one-inch needle plunged into her hip, to have her marrow extracted, or to donate her marrow to her older sister. She didn't agree to take the risks that go with any surgical procedure; she didn't agree to a procedure that was meant to benefit another, not her. Perhaps, when she became old enough to understand what her parents had done to her, she'd become resentful. Perhaps her parents would never love her as a child should be loved, for her own sake. Even worse, perhaps the Ayalas' success would inspire other parents in similar circumstances to conceive savior siblings. Perhaps eventually large numbers of children would be born solely for their organs. Such a cheapening of human life, the critics concluded, must never be permitted.

Defenders of the Ayalas responded forcefully. Couples, they pointed out, are permitted to have children for any reason, or for no reason at all. We can't, then, consistently condemn the Ayalas unless we condemn many other couples too. Furthermore, just because Marissa was conceived for Anissa's sake, it doesn't follow that the Ayalas wouldn't simultaneously love Marissa for her own sake. Nothing is wrong with using others as means, provided we treat them as ends at the same time – and clearly the Ayalas, while using Marissa as a means to saving Anissa's life, could also treat Marissa, provided only that they loved her, as an end in herself. Finally, although the surgical procedure that Marissa underwent posed some risks, the risks were only modest, whereas the potential benefit – saving Anissa's life – was incalculably great.

So who was right: the Ayalas' critics or the Ayalas' defenders? Is anything wrong with giving birth to savior siblings?

Postscript: More than a quarter of a century has passed since the bone marrow transplant. To this day, Anissa remains free of cancer. Marissa is now a college graduate, and enjoys a close relationship with her sister and parents. In an interview from 2011, she said, "People are entitled to their own opinions, but I am so glad that I am in this family. I could not have asked for a better family, so I've never questioned it." The Ayalas' story has encouraged some 100,000 people to volunteer for bone marrow donor lists.

Case Study 14
Autism and Vaccination

Jenny McCarthy

In 2005 Jenny McCarthy, an actor and former *Playboy* centerfold, received bad news: her son, Evan, was diagnosed with autism. Autism is one of a trio of related developmental disorders, the other members of the trio being Asperger syndrome and pervasive developmental disorder – not otherwise specified (PDD-NOS). These disorders, referred to collectively as autism spectrum disorders, are characterized by difficulties in learning language and in interacting with others. The symptoms usually manifest themselves before age three, and they can range from mild to severe. Those with more severe symptoms don't talk at all – that's roughly forty percent of all who suffer from an autism spectrum disorder. According to the Centers for Disease Control, one out of every 110 children has an autism spectrum disorder.

Like any good parent, McCarthy wanted to help her son. She searched for the cause of Evan's condition, and, more importantly, she searched for a cure. Eventually, she thought she found both. The cause, she claimed, was vaccination: "It's an infection and/or toxins and/or funguses on top of vaccines that push children into this neurological downslide which we call autism." And the cure, she said, included a special diet: "a gluten-free, casein-free diet, vitamin supplementation, detox of metals, and anti-fungals for yeast overgrowth." When she tried this cure on her son, Evan's condition improved. McCarthy conceded that, although the diet cured her son, it might not help every child with autism. Different things, she maintained, work for different children. Thus, she advised parents of autistic children to "try everything."

Was McCarthy right? Do vaccines cause autism? Can diet cure autism? A great many people think so. According to one survey, twenty-nine percent of Americans agree that "vaccines given to children are partly responsible for causing autism," while another study found that twenty-four percent of parents have "some trust" that celebrities like McCarthy provide accurate information about the harmful effects of vaccines. Could so many people be mistaken?

Do Vaccines Cause Autism?

There are several arguments for an affirmative answer to this question. All of the arguments, however, are flawed.

First argument: Normally the symptoms of autism make their appearance only after a child has had a number of vaccinations. If vaccinations come first and autism comes afterward, it stands to reason that vaccinations cause autism.

Flaw: The first argument commits a logical fallacy called *post hoc ergo propter hoc*, a Latin phrase that translates into English as "after this, therefore because of this." The mere fact that A happens *after* B doesn't imply that A happens *because* of B. Thus, I may eat my dinner *after* the stock market closes for the day, but I don't eat dinner *because* the stock market closes for the day. Or again, the trees dropped their leaves *after* the terrorist attacks of 9/11, but they didn't drop their leaves *because* of the terrorist attacks of 9/11. In like manner, Evan's autistic symptoms may have appeared only *after* Evan had his vaccinations, but it doesn't follow that the vaccinations *caused* the autistic symptoms. Any of a number of other things could have caused the autistic symptoms instead – Evan's genetic makeup, for example.

Second argument: A correlation exists between vaccines and autism – when vaccines were developed several decades ago and more and more children were vaccinated, the number of reported cases of autism increased. Therefore, the increase in vaccinations probably caused the increase in reported cases of autism.

First flaw: The argument assumes that a correlation, all by itself, reveals something about what causes what. This assumption, however, is false. Take, for instance, this correlation: over a period of years, a Midwestern town saw an increase in the number of people who attended church as well as an increase in the number of refrigerators that were stolen. What accounts for this strange correlation between churchgoing and refrigerator thefts? Did churchgoing cause refrigerator thefts ("Since everyone's in church, I now have a chance to break into people's empty homes and steal some refrigerators")? Did refrigerator thefts cause churchgoing ("Since I just stole a refrigerator, I'd better repent by going to church – I don't want to burn in hell")? As it turned out, it was neither of the above: the increase in churchgoing and the increase in refrigerator thefts were both caused by a third factor –

namely, population growth. As the population increased, more people went to church, and more people turned to a life of crime. Thus, just because two things, A and B, are correlated doesn't imply that A causes B. It could be that B causes A, or that some third thing, C, causes both A and B. Or possibly the correlation is just a coincidence. In the case of vaccines and reported cases of autism, all of these possibilities would have to be explored before reaching any conclusion.

Second flaw: The argument ignores the crucial distinction between *reported* and *actual* cases of autism. While, over the past few decades, the number of *reported* cases of autism has increased, the number of *actual* cases may have remained steady, or even decreased. This could be so for any number of reasons. For example, as doctors learned more about autism over time, they may have gotten better at diagnosing it, thereby increasing the number of reported, but not actual, cases. Or while at one time only "low-functioning" children were counted as autistic, these days "high-functioning" children can also count as autistic. Or perhaps the increase in special-education programs motivated parents to pressure doctors to give a diagnosis of autism. In circumstances such as these, even though a correlation exists between vaccines and *reported* cases of autism, a correlation may not exist between vaccines and *actual* cases of autism.

Third argument: In 1998 Dr. Andrew Wakefield and thirteen coauthors published an article in *The Lancet*. The article reported on twelve children in London's Royal Free Hospital, all of whom had autistic symptoms as well as intestinal problems – pain, bloating, and inflammation. In addition, eight of the dozen children had developed their autistic symptoms only days after receiving the MMR vaccine – that is, the triple vaccine that protects against measles, mumps, and rubella. Although the article never claimed that the vaccine causes autism, Wakefield, speaking for himself, suggested that the measles virus in the vaccine might trigger intestinal inflammation and that the intestinal inflammation might have an impact on brain development, thereby causing autism.

Flaw: After Wakefield's views became public, at least twenty-five studies, all of them published in peer-reviewed scientific journals, attempted to establish a causal link between the MMR vaccine and autism. None of them, however, succeeded. In 2004 ten of Wakefield's thirteen coauthors retracted their 1998 article, and in 2010 so did *The Lancet* – after the British General Medical Council found that Wakefield had violated ethical principles when gathering data for the article. The scientific community has thus rejected Wakefield's suggestion that the MMR vaccine causes autism.

Fourth argument: Starting in the 1930s, thimerosal, a mercury compound, was used in vaccines to prevent the growth of bacteria and mold. Mercury, however, can cause brain damage, especially in young children. According to a 2001 study released by the Food and Drug Administration, six-month-old babies who'd had all of the five recommended vaccinations were exposed to twice the levels of mercury that were held to be safe. It therefore seems reasonable that the thimerosal in vaccines causes autism.

Flaw: After the 2001 study was released, vaccine makers quickly produced versions of all five vaccines that were free of thimerosal. If, therefore, thimerosal caused autism, the rates of autism should have dropped once the thimerosal-free vaccines were available. This, though, didn't happen. As the National Institute of Medicine has concluded, "The evidence favors rejection of a causal relationship between thimerosal-containing vaccines and autism."

Fifth argument: As time has passed, more and more vaccinations have been recommended for children. But as the number of vaccines increases, so does the number of antigens to which children are exposed. All of these antigens can overwhelm a child's immune system, leading to autism.

Flaw: One of the premises of the argument is false. The increase in the number of vaccines has not meant an increase in the number of antigens. For example, in 1980 the smallpox vaccine that was given to children contained two hundred antigens. By contrast, today all of the standardly given vaccines combined contain only one hundred fifty antigens.

The scientific evidence is consequently overwhelming: vaccines don't cause autism. But if vaccines don't cause autism, what does? Nobody knows, though autism appears to have a genetic component. It is known, for example, that if one identical twin has autism, the other also has it between sixty and ninety percent of the time, and siblings of an autistic person are twenty-five times more likely to have autism than the population at large.

Can Diet Cure Autism?

After McCarthy fed her son a gluten-free, casein-free diet, Evan's condition improved. McCarthy concluded that the diet caused the improvement. McCarthy's reasoning, however, is another example of *post hoc ergo propter hoc*. The mere fact that Evan's improvement came *after* the change in his diet doesn't imply that Evan improved *because* of the new diet.

Could something other than the new diet have caused Evan's improvement? Yes. As Christopher Chabris and Daniel Simons, authors of *The Invisible Gorilla*, write:

> Given the overwhelming scientific evidence that autism has strong genetic bases and that brain development in people with autism differs markedly from brain development in typical children, it's more likely that Evan's improvements resulted from extensive behavioral modification therapy that does help some children with autism. Or perhaps his symptoms just became less pronounced as he matured. It's even possible that Evan did not have autism in the first place, but instead had another disorder with similar symptoms that could have improved in response to medicines he was given for seizures.

The consensus within the scientific community is that diet almost certainly won't cure autism. On the contrary, autism is a lifelong condition that has no cure.

A Moral Dilemma

When asked whether parents should vaccinate their children, McCarthy answered, "If I had another child, there's no way in hell." Many parents feel the same way McCarthy does. Some believe, with McCarthy, that vaccinations cause autism or other health problems. Others believe that measles and other diseases are a part of childhood, that they strengthen a child's immune system, or that they are God's will. For these reasons, close to one in eight parents have refused at least one vaccination for their children, and approximately six percent of children enter school without any vaccinations at all. At present, U.S. law permits this: forty-five states waive vaccinations when parents object to them on religious grounds, and fifteen states allow parents to seek waivers on personal philosophical grounds.

But some people argue that the laws should be more restrictive. When children don't receive, say, the MMR vaccine, they're at an elevated risk of getting measles, mumps, or rubella. They could die. In addition, they could infect other people who also haven't been vaccinated. According to Paul Offit, an expert on viruses, "There are 500,000 people in the United States who can't be vaccinated. They can't be vaccinated because they're on cancer chemotherapy, or they've had a bone marrow transplant, or a solid organ transplant, or they're receiving steroids because they have severe asthma. They depend on those around them being vaccinated." The consequences of allowing parents not to have their children vaccinated are thus potentially serious. The Centers for Disease Control, attempting to quantify the seriousness of failure to vaccinate, estimates that vaccinating every U.S. child born in a given year from birth to adolescence prevents fourteen million infections, saves thirty-three thousand lives, and saves ten billion dollars in health care costs.

So what should be done? Should parents have the freedom to decide for themselves whether or not their children are vaccinated? Or should the government step in and require vaccinations for all children who can be vaccinated?

Case Study 15
Medical Science versus Christian Science

The problems for two-year-old Robyn Twitchell began on April 3, 1986. Shortly after eating a light supper, the little boy started to cry, and then to vomit and scream. Concerned, his parents, David and Ginger, sought help.

Mr. and Mrs. Twitchell were Christian Scientists living in Boston, the birthplace of their religion. Christian Science teaches that disease has no physical being, but on the contrary is the absence of being. Since God is complete being, disease is the absence of God. Ill people, then, are estranged from God. Consequently, to cure an ill person is to restore that person's relationship with God. For this reason, Christian Science practitioners don't prescribe drugs or perform surgery – these won't help patients understand the spiritual source of their illness. Instead, Christian Science practitioners rely on teaching, discussion, and prayer.

In accordance with their religious beliefs, Mr. and Mrs. Twitchell contacted a Christian Science practitioner. The practitioner visited Robyn three times in five days, praying for him and singing hymns. A Christian Scientist nurse was also on hand to feed and bathe the young child. According to one account, Robyn's condition appeared to alternate between improving and getting worse again. In the end, though, it worsened. On April 8, five days after the onset of his symptoms, Robyn started to have spasms and his eyes rolled up in his head. He lost consciousness and during the evening he died.

As it turned out, Robyn died of a bowel obstruction. According to the doctors who examined the dead child, the bowel obstruction could have been treated with surgery and medicine. The little boy, they were certain, didn't have to die.

The state of Massachusetts charged the Twitchells with involuntary manslaughter; the trial lasted two months. The defense appealed to the First Amendment, arguing that the Twitchells had a constitutionally guaranteed right to the free expression of their religion. By prosecuting them, the state was violating this right.

The prosecution rejected this argument. The First Amendment, the prosecutors pointed out, admits of exceptions. There are laws banning polygamy, for example, even though some religions endorse the practice, and there are laws requiring blood transfusions for minors, despite protests from Jehovah's Witnesses. The courts have found such laws to be consistent with the Constitution.

Furthermore, according to the prosecutors, the Twitchells, by failing to seek proper medical care for their son, had violated Robyn's rights. In support of this contention, the prosecutors quoted the famous line from the 1923 Supreme Court decision in *Prince v. Massachusetts*: "Parents may make martyrs of themselves, but it does not follow that they are free, in identical circumstances, to make martyrs of their children."

The jury found the Twitchells guilty; the judge sentenced them to ten years of probation. Among the requirements of their probation: the Twitchells had to seek medical care for their three surviving children if the children needed it, and the Twitchells had to bring their children to a physician for regular checkups.

John Kiernan, representing the prosecution, hailed the decision. It was "a victory for children," he said. "The message has been sent. Every parent of whatever religious belief or persuasion is obligated to include medical care in taking care of his or her child."

But not everyone agreed with the decision. According to Stephen Lyons, one of the defense attorneys, it was a mistake to "substitute the imperfect and flawed judgment of medicine for the judgment of a parent." A spokesperson for the Christian Science church said, "They're trying to prosecute out of existence [the Christian Science] method of treatment." To this, David Twitchell added, "This has been a prosecution against our faith."

During the trial, however, Mr. Twitchell had testified that "If medicine could have saved [Robyn], I wish I had turned to it." He also admitted during the trial that he once had had a toothache, and, when it didn't go away despite his prayers, he sought out a dentist, who gave him Novocain and performed root canal surgery. Mrs. Twitchell, too, had accepted painkillers when she gave birth. Why, then, hadn't the Twitchells considered medicine or surgery for their son? The answer is that, because Robyn's condition appeared to alternate between improving and getting worse, the Twitchells believed that their prayers were the cause of the improvements and hence that, in Robyn's case, Christian Science healing practices were effective.

Should the Twitchells have been found guilty of involuntary manslaughter? Was their sentence too harsh? Was it too lenient? Should the Christian Science approach to healing be respected? Should it be outlawed?

Postscript: Robyn Twitchell wasn't the only child of Christian Science parents to die due to lack of medical attention. In 1984 Natalie Middleton-Rippberger died of meningitis; in 1986 Amy Hermanson died of diabetes; in 1987 Elizabeth King died from a tumor that had ballooned to the size of two watermelons; in 1989 Ian Lundman died after developing a fever and losing weight. This list continues into the 1990s and the first two decades of the twenty-first century. Some of the parents of the dead children, like the Twitchells, were prosecuted, and some were found guilty. But none of them, also like the Twitchells, ever went to prison. The Twitchells appealed their conviction, and in 1993 they won the appeal because of the "special circumstances" of their case – namely, that they weren't permitted to introduce as evidence a booklet produced by their church called *Legal Rights and Obligations of Christian Scientists in Massachusetts*. The appeals court, however, affirmed "a common law duty to provide medical services for a child, the breach of which can be the basis, in the appropriate circumstances, for the conviction of a parent for involuntary manslaughter."

Christian Scientists aren't the only ones who reject medical treatment for religious reasons. The children of parents of other denominations – such as the Church of the First Born, the Faith Assembly, and the True Followers of Christ – also sometimes die due to lack of medical attention. Unlike Christian Science parents, however, who tend to be middle- or upper-class and well respected in their communities, the parents of other denominations have sometimes served prison sentences.

Case Study 16
The Vegan Baby

On July 31, 2000, Silva Swinton gave birth to a daughter in her Queens, New York, home, which she and her husband, Joseph, shared with relatives. No doctor was present, nor even a midwife, because Silva distrusted medical personnel and the American health care system. According to Silva, the birth proceeded smoothly: "I squatted and she came right out. Three pushes." The baby, however, was born three months premature, weighed only three pounds, and, as often happens with prematurely born babies, had a lung disorder. Silva and Joseph named the girl IIce (pronounced "Ice") Wings Swinton.

Rather than take the ailing girl to a doctor, Silva and Joseph treated her themselves. The key, they thought, was diet. Silva and Joseph were both vegans, at least in part for health reasons. At one time in her life, Silva weighed nearly 300 lb., but, after switching to a vegan diet and becoming more active, she lost 177 lb. If a vegan diet improved her health, she and her husband reasoned, perhaps it would improve IIce's health as well.

Can a vegan diet be healthy for a baby? Yes. Most vegan parents who wish their children to follow in their footsteps have no objections to breastfeeding. Human milk, they believe, is importantly different from cow's milk – unlike cows, for example, human mothers freely consent to give their milk. If breastfeeding isn't an option, vegan parents can use a commercially produced soy formula that the American Medical Association has approved. Silva, however, didn't breastfeed IIce, and she abandoned soy formula when, after four months of using it, IIce became "mucousy." This was when Silva started carefully reading the nutritional information provided on jars of baby food and spent a considerable sum of money on organic ingredients, which she pureed and fed to IIce. One of her homemade concoctions, which she claimed IIce loved, consisted of coconut milk, hazelnuts, pecans, ground soybeans, and an abundance of herbs, among which were slippery elm and Echinacea. The only animal product that IIce consumed was cod liver oil. Unfortunately, the little girl didn't thrive on the foods she ate. In November 2001, when she was fifteen months old, IIce weighed only ten pounds, not even half of what a fifteen-month-old should weigh.

Receiving an anonymous tip, the local Administration for Children's Services sent an agent to the Swintons' home to check on IIce. On November 16, 2001, IIce was taken to a hospital to be examined. Doctors found that she had a distended belly – a sign of severe malnutrition – as well as lanugo (fine hair covering the body), rickets, broken bones, and other internal injuries. Her hair was dirty and matted, her fingernails were so long they more closely resembled claws than fingernails, and she had, as one doctor put it, "the worst diaper rash you ever saw." She had no teeth, couldn't talk, and couldn't sit up. She may have suffered from neurological damage caused by poor nutrition. According to one doctor, she looked like a victim of "a famine in a far-off country." Another said that she was "at a severe and critical risk of dying." The Swintons had provided IIce with neither prenatal nor postnatal care, and had refused to give her any vaccinations. When the Queens district attorney learned what had happened, he said it was one of the worst cases of neglect he had ever come across. His office charged the Swintons with first-degree assault, first-degree reckless endangerment, and endangering the welfare of a child, charges serious enough to put the Swintons in jail for as much as twenty-five years, if convicted.

The Swintons pleaded not guilty. Bail was set at $20,000 for Silva and $20,000 for Joseph. Silva was able to post her bail, but Joseph couldn't, and thus he remained imprisoned at Rikers Island until the trial. In July 2002, while still awaiting trial, Silva gave birth to a son, InI (pronounced I-en-I). She hid him from authorities for fifteen days, but, when discovered, the boy, like his sister, was taken from his mother and placed with relatives. Both children were fed a medically prescribed vegan diet, which helped improve IIce's health. Silva was allowed regular visits with her children.

The trial began at the end of March 2003. The Swintons' defense rested on three contentions:

1) Silva and Joseph did not place IIce in imminent danger of dying. The defense pointed out that on November 6, 2001, ten days before IIce was taken to the hospital, an emergency medical technician who visited the Swintons' home reported that IIce, although small, was otherwise in good health. The following day, a social worker examined IIce and saw no reason to remove her. Taking the stand at her trial, Silva testified that IIce was a "good eater" who was able to crawl and babble and "walk in her walker." When she was shown a photograph, taken at the hospital, of IIce with a distended belly and spindly arms and legs, Silva replied, "That's not my child. That's not how she looked when she was with me." Silva argued that IIce lost her ability to sit up and support her head only after she was taken to the hospital, as a result of complications from a brain scan that the doctors had ordered. A pediatrician testifying on behalf of the defense, Dr. Gary Brown, agreed that it was hospital staff, not the Swintons, who put IIce's life in danger, claiming that, with her breathing problems, IIce should not have been sedated for exams. When pressed, Silva admitted that, as a nutritionist had explained to her, IIce's diet should have contained more calcium and fat, but she insisted that IIce thrived on her vegan diet. But if she thrived on her vegan diet, the prosecuting attorney asked her, why was IIce so lethargic at the hospital? In response, Silva suggested that this was IIce's way of resisting medical treatment: "She was fighting." When the prosecuting attorney scoffed at the idea of a tiny infant resisting medical treatment, Silva replied, "You're kind of small yourself, Mr. Rosenbaum."

2) *The health problems IIce had when she was with the Swintons resulted from her premature birth and lung disorder, not anything the Swintons did.* Contradicting all the doctors and nutritionists who testified for the prosecution, Dr. Brown claimed that IIce's premature birth and lung disorder caused her to develop rickets and developmental delays. Her diet, he said, was not an issue.

3) *Silva and Joseph meant well.* To be found guilty of first-degree assault, someone must have depraved intentions. According to the defense, however, Silva and Joseph didn't have depraved intentions. On the contrary, they loved IIce and did what they believed was best for her. Silva, for example, wouldn't have gone to the expense and trouble of making organic homemade baby food unless she meant well. But, the prosecution countered, Silva and Joseph must – or at least should – have noticed that, in spite of their efforts, IIce remained in poor health. If they meant well, why didn't they take further steps to improve her health? To address this question, the defense called on a psychologist who testified that Joseph had only a seventh-grade education and an IQ of 78, which put him on the border of mental retardation. Someone like that, the defense maintained, might genuinely not have understood how serious IIce's poor health was. Silva, by contrast, was highly articulate and had taken a number of college-level courses. Yet she, too, claimed not to know the full extent of IIce's

health problems. She thought, for example, that IIce's bowed legs, which were in fact caused by rickets, simply meant that IIce was double jointed, and she thought IIce's lanugo was nothing more than hairiness that she inherited from her mother, who was also hairy. She had read that, at its first birthday, a baby should weigh three times as much as it did at birth, and, when IIce was a year old, she weighed nine pounds, three times what she weighed when she was born. From this, Silva concluded that IIce's growth was on a normal trajectory and that IIce was reasonably healthy.

On April 4, the jury of nine women and three men, all of whom had experience raising children and none of whom was vegan or vegetarian, found the Swintons guilty of all charges. Some black advocacy groups, concerned that children were taken from black families at a higher rate than from white families, suspected that the verdict was racist, as Silva and Joseph were black and the jury was mostly white. Silva was sentenced to six years in prison and Joseph to five years. In July 2006, three years into their sentences, the judge threw out the first-degree assault verdict and released the couple from prison. The couple were hopeful that they'd be able to reunite with their two children.

Was the first-degree assault conviction justified? How free should parents be to raise their children as they see fit? Is anything wrong with raising a child on a vegan diet?

Part 3
RESEARCHERS AND SUBJECTS

Case Study 17
Bad Blood

On May 16, 1997, in a White House ceremony, President Bill Clinton issued a formal apology on behalf of the nation. "What the United States did was shameful," he said, "and I am sorry." The apology was for violating the rights, over a period of four decades, of 399 African-American men who suffered from syphilis. By the time Clinton apologized, only a handful of them were still alive.

The events that culminated in Clinton's apology began in 1930, when the United States Public Health Service (PHS) launched a program in Macon County, Alabama, to diagnose and treat 10,000 African Americans for syphilis. The program, though well intentioned, proved overly ambitious. Testing revealed that 35% of African Americans living in Macon County were infected with the disease, a much higher percentage than was anticipated, so that treating everyone would have been a daunting task even with proper funding. But with the Great Depression underway, funding for programs like this was scarce. By 1931, the money for the program ran out. Only 1,400 people received even partial treatment.

Unable to treat any more patients, the PHS settled for conducting a six-month observational study, the cost of which was minimal. Working with the Tuskegee Institute, and getting assistance from black churches and community leaders, the PHS recruited participants for the study. The goal of the study was to determine the effects of untreated syphilis on African-American men. At the time, nobody knew very well what these effects were. Many believed – incorrectly, we now know – that syphilis had lesser effects on black Americans than on white Americans. If the observational study could yield more accurate knowledge of the effects of syphilis, physicians might be able – when funding once again became available – to provide more appropriate treatment. The study eventually came to involve 600 participants, 399 of whom had syphilis. The remaining 201 participants served as a control group.

The 399 men with syphilis, living in an impoverished part of the country and having little income and little education, knew next to nothing about health care. They knew from their symptoms that something was wrong with their health, but they didn't know what condition they had. Instead of informing them that they had syphilis, those conducting the study told them they had "bad blood." The participants were also told that they were receiving effective treatment when in fact they were given placebos. According to the PHS, "bad blood" was the term African Americans living in Macon County used for syphilis, but this was misleading. In reality, it was a catchall phrase that covered many conditions, including syphilis, but also including, for example, iron deficiency, sickle-cell disease, leukemia, and low energy. Thus, although the participants in the study all consented to their participation, their consent was less than fully informed.

At the end of the six months, the PHS learned that syphilis was just as deadly among black Americans as it was among white Americans. Hoping to learn more, the PHS extended the study – and kept on extending it, year after year after year.

In 1938, six years into the study, the United States passed the National Venereal Disease Control Act, which required the PHS to treat people suffering from syphilis. The PHS, however, chose not to treat the 399 men, on the grounds that, as participants in a scientific study, they weren't subject to the requirements of the law.

In 1947, fifteen years into the study, the Nuremberg Code was formulated. A response to the discovery of atrocities committed by Nazi experimenters, the Nuremberg Code set forth the basic rights that participants in scientific studies should be accorded. According to the Nuremberg Code, for a scientific study to be ethically justified, all human subjects must give their consent, their consent must be fully free, and their consent must be fully informed. Although the Tuskegee syphilis study clearly violated the Nuremberg Code, given that the participants weren't fully informed, the PHS allowed the study to continue.

In 1969, thirty-seven years into the study, the Centers for Disease Control (CDC) convened a panel to review the study. With only one dissenting member, the panel recommended that the study continue, arguing that treatment at such a late stage might cause more harm than good.

In 1972, forty years into the study, Jean Heller, a reporter for the Associated Press, discovering how the participants of the study were being treated, published her findings. The ensuing national outrage was what finally put an end to the study. By that time, twenty-eight of the participants had died from syphilis, another hundred had died from related complications, forty spouses had been infected, and nineteen children had been born with the disease.

Today, as in 1972, Americans are outraged when they learn about the Tuskegee syphilis study. For us today, the puzzle isn't whether the study was or wasn't morally justified. We overwhelmingly agree that it wasn't, and we might suspect that such an egregious violation of human rights could have happened only in a deeply racist society, that nothing of the sort would have happened had the participants been white instead of black. Still, the Tuskegee syphilis study raises a number of enormously difficult – and fundamental – questions about human rights. Here are a few of them.

1) What are human rights? Human rights advocates think of human rights as trump – they take precedence over other things that people value. If, for example, I have a right to life, you may not kill me, even if thousands of people hate my guts, so that my death would bring them great joy. Similarly, if I have a right to property, you may not steal my life savings, even if you donate the money to a charitable organization and the charitable organization uses the money to save thousands of lives. When the PHS conducted its study, it was with the hope of acquiring knowledge about the effects of syphilis, knowledge that could be used to save lives. Saving lives has great value. But what the PHS failed to recognize was that the rights of the participants in the study – as well as the rights of their families – should have taken precedence. We mustn't sacrifice the rights of a few hundred, or even one, to save the lives of thousands or millions. That, according to human rights advocates, is how powerful rights are.

But why should this be? Why should the rights of an individual trump the well-being of a society? Why isn't it the other way around, the well-being of a society trumping the rights of an individual? Because a society is larger than an individual, isn't it more valuable? Indeed, some philosophers, maintaining that societal well-being takes precedence over the individual, reject the notion of human rights. Jeremy Bentham (1748-1832), for example, famously derided human rights as "nonsense upon stilts" – although the notion appears elevated and noble, it's ultimately groundless, he thought.

2) Who has human rights? The answer to this question would seem to be obvious – those who have human rights are human beings. As human beings, the participants in the Tuskegee syphilis study had rights. The color of their skin didn't matter. Neither did their poverty or lack of education. Only their humanity mattered. By treating them as little more than laboratory animals, by acting as if they were less than fully human, the PHS violated their rights.

But why should humanity matter? Humanity is simply the biological fact of being a member of the species *Homo sapiens*. But why should this biological fact – but not skin color, which is also a biological fact – be relevant to having rights? If skin color, gender, eye color, the number of bones in one's hand, and other biological facts don't endow someone with rights, why should humanity? Perhaps, we might think, humanity matters because only human beings are able to understand rights, and it's this ability that gives human beings rights. Or perhaps humanity matters because only human beings are highly intelligent, or use language, or develop cultures. But none of this can be right, for the simple reason that some human beings – newborn babies and the very severely brain-damaged, for example – don't understand rights, aren't highly intelligent, don't use language, and don't develop cultures. Yet they, it seems, should be accorded rights just like any other human being. What feature or features, then, did the participants in the Tuskegee syphilis study have that endowed them with rights?

3) What rights do human beings have? Different writers provide different lists of rights. Take, for example, these four lists:

- John Locke (1632-1704): life, liberty, and property
- The Declaration of Independence (1776): life, liberty, and the pursuit of happiness
- The Universal Declaration of Human Rights (1948): life, liberty, and security of the person
- Tom Regan (1938-2017): life, liberty, and bodily integrity

One of the rights common to all four lists is the right to life. We might think this was the right that the PHS violated since so many of the syphilitic men died when they could have been saved. But what does it mean to have a right to life? On one plausible interpretation, a right to life is nothing more than a right not to be killed. But if this is what a right to life is, the PHS didn't violate anyone's right to life – they allowed a number of people to die, to be sure, but they didn't kill anybody. It was syphilis, not the PHS, that killed the participants in the study. Allowing to die might be a bad thing, maybe, as some philosophers believe, as bad as killing, but it's not the same thing as killing.

But perhaps a right to life means something else. Perhaps it means a right to be given the minimum one needs to survive. If this is right, the PHS violated the syphilitic men's right to life, because it failed to give these men the treatment they needed to continue living. The problem, though, is that this conception of a right to life is highly controversial. It implies, for example, that the sick have a right to receive health care, whether they can afford it or not. Although the National Venereal Disease Control Act of 1938, which required the PHS to treat people suffering from syphilis, is consistent with such a right, such a right would require the government – that is, taxpayers – to pay for the healthcare of the poor. Yet taxpayers have rights too, and requiring them to spend their hard-earned money on the health care of those whose illness they didn't cause seems to be a violation of their rights.

The upshot of all this is that, while the Tuskegee syphilis study seems clearly wrong, exactly what makes it wrong is difficult to pin down. So what makes it wrong? Did the PHS violate anyone's right to life? What are human rights? Who has human rights? Which rights do human beings have?

Case Study 18
Prison Experiments

During World War II, the U.S. military carried out a wide range of research projects – for example, testing survival clothing, grafting skin, exploring nutritional deficiencies, treating malaria and dysentery, and seeking a substitute for human blood to be used in transfusions. Finding volunteers to participate in these studies, however, wasn't easy, since large numbers of men were needed for military service and large numbers of women were needed in the workforce. The U.S. military therefore turned to prisons. Prisoners volunteered for the experiments readily enough – volunteering was a way to express patriotism. By the end of the war, prison experimentation had become an established practice.

Around this time, pharmaceutical companies started using prisoners to test new drugs – especially during Phase I clinical trials. In Phase I trials, the first phase of human testing, drugs are tested for side effects and safe dosage, but aren't yet tested for effectiveness. Since the testing that takes place at this early stage doesn't aim to benefit those on whom the drug is tested, people are often reluctant to volunteer to participate in Phase I trials. From the standpoint of the pharmaceutical industry, the use of prisoners conveniently solved this problem. (For a description of all the phases of a clinical trial, see Table 1 at the end of this case study.)

Prison experiments continued to be common into the 1970s – "until the early 1970s," said one researcher, "about ninety percent of new drugs were first tested on prison inmates." Here are some examples of prison experiments conducted between the early 1940s and the early 1970s:

- During the Second World War, the U.S. military conducted a transfusion study in which sixty-four prisoners were injected with filtered beef blood. Twenty of the prisoners became ill from an immune reaction, and one died.
- In 1944 researchers from the University of Chicago, working on behalf of the U.S. Army, infected five hundred healthy

Illinois State Penitentiary inmates with malaria. The purpose of the study was to test how effective several drugs were in lowering the rate of relapse among malaria sufferers. The study was claimed to be important because much of the Second World War was fought in parts of the world that were plagued by malaria, but the results of the study weren't published until 1946, after the war ended.

- During the 1950s researchers exposed the testicles of one hundred thirty Oregon and Washington prisoners to radiation. The researchers wished to learn about the effects of radiation on reproductive tissue.
- In 1963 researchers injected Ohio and Illinois prisoners with blood from leukemia patients. The researchers wanted to determine whether leukemia could be transmitted.
- During the Cold War, in Holmesburg State Prison in Pennsylvania, the U.S. Army gave inmates various doses of LSD and six other powerful mind-altering drugs. The goal of the study was to find the minimum dose of these drugs that would disable half the people receiving it. With this knowledge, the military could put the drug in, for instance, a city's water supply, thereby incapacitating the inhabitants.
- Also in Holmesburg State Prison, prisoners were used to test a variety of skin products, such as creams, moisturizers, shampoos, and deodorants. Some prisoners were also exposed to radiation and chemicals, including dioxin, a component of Agent Orange, a defoliant that was heavily used during the war in Vietnam and was suspected of causing neurological disorders and cancers.
- In 1970 Robert E. Hodges withheld ascorbic acid from Iowa State Prison inmates. Five of the inmates developed scurvy. This result merely confirmed what scientists already knew about the absence of ascorbic acid in people's diet.

The prisoners who participated in these experiments all had a choice. If they hadn't wanted to participate, they didn't have to. But they wanted to participate, and so gave their consent. However, by the 1970s, many philosophers, lawmakers, and researchers maintained that giving consent wasn't by itself enough to make an experiment ethically justified. In addition, the consent needed to be fully *informed*, and it needed to be fully *free* – and this was true of the consent given by *any* human beings used as subjects in an experiment, even prisoners convicted of heinous crimes.

First, was the consent of the prisoners who participated in experiments between 1940 and the early 1970s fully informed? In many cases, arguably not. Many of the prisoners either couldn't read at all or could only barely read. To understand what an experiment was about and what the risks were, they had to rely on explanations given orally by the experimenters. But the experimenters' explanations may have been biased, in order to encourage prisoners' consent.

Second, was the consent of the prisoners fully free? In many cases, arguably not. Life in prison was routine, the environment boring. Even small luxuries were absent, and the threat of violence was constant. Participation in an experiment might have been a welcome change of pace – prisoners would spend time in the comfort and safety of a clinic, they'd get frequent personal attention from the experimenters, and they'd enjoy better food. In addition, they might get an earlier release from prison, and they were often paid up to $300 or $400 a month. This contrasted with the pay – between $4.50 and $7.50 a month – that they received for working in the prison's industries, making clothes, for example, or doing carpentry. Under these circumstances, a prisoner's decision to participate in an experiment, and assume risks he otherwise wouldn't have assumed, may have been less than fully free.

As a result of concerns such as these, Institutional Review Boards (IRBs) were set up and instructed to protect the rights of prisoners serving as experimental subjects. Starting in 1978 IRBs were required to follow four guidelines regulating federally funded prison experiments:

1. Compensation for participation in research should not be coercive. In a prison setting, even the opportunity to eat better food could be coercive.
2. The risks of participating in an experiment should be acceptable to potential subjects who aren't prisoners.
3. Prisoners who choose not to participate shouldn't be denied parole or privileges they'd otherwise be entitled to.
4. When the research is complete, subjects should be provided with medical care for any condition they may have acquired as a result of the research.

Two further guidelines were added in 2001:

5. At least one member of the IRB must either be a prisoner or represent prisoners.
6. The majority of IRB members who aren't prisoners must have no association with the prison.

Some argue that these guidelines, though a step in the right direction, don't go far enough. For example, the guidelines apply only to federally funded research. But shouldn't they also apply to privately funded research? Furthermore, the guidelines define a prisoner narrowly, as someone who is in a prison (about two million people). But what about those who are on probation or parole (about five million people)? Like prisoners defined narrowly, people on probation or parole are a vulnerable group. Don't they deserve the same protections as those who are in a prison?

Others, however, argue that the guidelines go too far. People are in prison because they've committed crimes. They've violated the rights of law-abiding citizens. Because they've violated the rights of others, they should lose their own rights. Participating in risky experiments may be seen as part of the punishment that criminals have coming to them. Prisoners should have no choice in the matter; obtaining their free and informed consent shouldn't be required.

So who is right? Under what circumstances may prisoners be used in research?

Table 1: Clinical Trial Phases

New drugs, surgical procedures, and other therapies are tested in a sequence of four phases. Animal testing is commonly done before Phase I testing begins, although further animal testing may be done while human studies are underway.	
Phase I	Researchers test the therapy in a small number of people (20-80). The trial evaluates the safety and identifies the side effects of the therapy, and, if the therapy is a drug, the trial determines the range of a safe dose. The trial does not aim to test the effectiveness of the therapy.
Phase II	Researchers test the therapy in a larger group of people (100-300). The aim of the trial is to determine how effective the therapy is and to further test the safety of the therapy.
Phase III	Researchers test the therapy in an even larger number of people (1,000-3,000). The trial aims to confirm the effectiveness of the therapy, monitor its side effects, and compare it with accepted therapies. Researchers also collect data for improving the therapy and increasing its safety.
Phase IV	Researchers collect data about the effects of the therapy after the therapy has become a standard treatment. The goal is to refine the use of the therapy and increase its safety.

Case Study 19
Huntington's Disease – and Beyond

Huntington's disease is caused by a single gene. If one of your parents carries the gene, there's a fifty percent chance that you too will carry the gene, and, if you do, you'll get the disease. Nothing you can do will keep you safe. No matter how much you exercise, no matter what you eat, no matter what medications you take – the disease will come. It won't come right away, though. For the first thirty-five or forty-five years of your life, you'll feel perfectly healthy. Then, when the symptoms finally arrive, they'll develop only gradually. You may scarcely notice them at first – a small facial twitch, a slight slur in your speech, an occasional clumsiness, a bit of moodiness. But the symptoms will get worse. Before the disease runs its course, you can expect to experience hallucinations, emotional outbursts, paranoia, uncontrollable grimaces, an unsteady gait, wild jerking of the arms and legs, loss of memory, and depression. There is no effective treatment for the disease, and it's invariably fatal. From the onset of the symptoms, you might live fifteen or twenty more years – if, that is, you don't, out of sheer hopelessness, commit suicide first.

In 1968, after his wife was diagnosed with Huntington's disease, Milton Wexler founded the Hereditary Disease Foundation. His hope was that the Foundation might find a cure for Huntington's, in case either of his daughters, Alice and Nancy, inherited the Huntington's gene. Nancy, the younger of Milton's daughters, earned her Ph.D. in clinical psychology in 1974, but, taking an interest in the disease that afflicted her mother, turned away from psychology and became a geneticist instead. Working with the Hereditary Disease Foundation, Nancy led a group of scientists to Lake Maracaibo in Venezuela. In this remote location lived a large family many of whose members – about 100 – had Huntington's, and many more – about 1,100 – were at risk of developing it. Nancy and her team collected a family history and took blood and skin samples for analysis. By 1993, thanks to the work that Nancy, as well as many others, had done, the Huntington's gene was finally located near the tip of chromosome 4. Soon afterward, a test for the presence of the gene was developed. No cure had yet been found, but anyone who had a family history of Huntington's could take the test and find out whether she or he carried the Huntington's gene.

Alice and Nancy had always assumed that, should such a test be developed, they would take it. But now that the test had been developed, they were no longer so sure. What, after all, would be the point of taking the test? Suppose the test revealed that they had the gene. What good would the knowledge do? They'd still develop the symptoms, slowly deteriorate, and eventually die – and their father, knowing their fate and unable to change it, would be devastated. Perhaps ignorance is sometimes for the best.

On the other hand, taking the test may have advantages. First, it might help those with a family history of Huntington's make more appropriate long-term plans: "I was hoping to retire at sixty-seven and then travel the world, but now that I know I have the Huntington's gene, I think I'll travel this summer, while I'm still healthy"; or "I was going to travel abroad this summer, but now that I know I don't have the Huntington's gene, I think I'll wait until I retire, when I'll be better able to afford it."

Second, taking the test may help prospective marriage partners make a more informed decision about whether to say "I do." Taking care of a spouse with Huntington's is a tremendous burden. While some prospective marriage partners may cheerfully accept the burden, others may prefer to be with someone healthier.

Finally, taking the test may help couples, one of whom has a family history of Huntington's, decide whether or not to have children. If the test comes up negative, the couple can be confident that their children will be free of the disease; if the test comes up positive, the couple will know that any child they conceive will have a fifty percent chance of inheriting the Huntington's gene. The couple may opt to have children in the former case, but not the latter.

Suppose the test comes up positive, but the couple still opts to have a child. The woman becomes pregnant; the couple is concerned about the health of the fetus. The test for the Huntington's gene can be used in conjunction with amniocentesis to determine whether the fetus will develop Huntington's disease. Should the couple have their fetus tested? If they have their fetus tested and the test comes up positive, would it be morally permissible for the couple to get an abortion and then try to have another, healthier child?[2]

---

[2] Case Study 9 addresses this question in greater detail.

Alternatively, if the couple wishes to avoid an abortion, they could try in vitro fertilization (IVF). Suppose several of the woman's eggs are fertilized with the man's sperm, and each resulting embryo is then tested for the Huntington's gene. Suppose further that all but one of the embryos have the gene; the remaining embryo doesn't. Wouldn't it be best – maybe even morally required – to implant the embryo that's missing the Huntington's gene, and then destroy the other embryos?

Similar questions arise in connection with conditions other than Huntington's disease. What about, for example, asthma? Admittedly, asthma differs from Huntington's disease in important ways. For one, it's usually not fatal – although it can be – and, for another, there isn't a single gene that seals the asthma sufferer's fate. Still, asthma, like Huntington's, negatively affects one's quality of life, and one can have a genetic predisposition to develop asthma. Suppose, then, that researchers discover a cluster of genes that predispose one to get asthma, and suppose a test is devised, similar to the test for the Huntington's gene, that allows couples who opt for IVF to determine whether a given embryo has this cluster of genes. If two embryos, as far as the best genetic testing can determine, are equally healthy, except that one has a genetic predisposition to develop asthma while the other doesn't, which embryo should the couple choose? For the sake of the well-being of their child, shouldn't they choose the embryo that doesn't have a genetic predisposition to develop asthma, just as they should choose the embryo that won't develop Huntington's disease?

Perhaps more controversial are non-disease traits such as intelligence. Like asthma and Huntington's disease, intelligence appears to have a genetic component and it appears to affect one's quality of life. According to one study, for instance, the people who are most likely to describe themselves as happy have an IQ between 120 and 129, well above the average of 100, whereas the people who are least likely to describe themselves as happy have an IQ between 70 and 79. To explain this finding, the authors of the study hypothesized that more intelligent people are more easily able than less intelligent people to acquire the knowledge they need to maintain their well-being and good health. Thus far, researchers haven't identified any cluster of intelligence genes, nor have they devised any test to detect them. But perhaps one day they will. If they do, shouldn't couples choose an embryo predisposed to greater intelligence, for the same reason they should choose an embryo not predisposed to get asthma – namely, that the resulting child will likely have a higher quality of life? In fact, won't choosing for higher intelligence likely result in a higher quality of life not just for the child but for others too? Highly intelligent people, we might argue, can benefit society in ways that the less intelligent can't. Finding cures for diseases, inventing new technologies, catching elusive terrorists – all of these take intelligence, and all of these improve quality of life for everyone. There seem to be many good reasons to select for intelligence.

Or are there? Could selecting for intelligence be going too far – perhaps because it's playing God, perhaps because it's interfering with nature, perhaps because it will create two classes of people, the enhanced and the unenhanced, with the former having an unfair advantage over the latter? Should some genetic research remain undone? Where should we draw the line between what's permissible and what's not?

Postscript: Alice and Nancy Wexler have declined to reveal whether they have taken the test for the Huntington's gene. Their reason is that they don't want other people to be influenced by the choice they happened to make. One thing, though, is clear: neither sister has the Huntington's gene. For both are well beyond the age when the symptoms of Huntington's become manifest, and both are still healthy.

Case Study 20
The Baby and the Baboon

Stephanie Fae Beauclair, better known as Baby Fae, was born on October 14, 1984, with hypoplastic left heart syndrome (HLHS). This defect, in which the left side of the heart is underdeveloped, is rare, occurring between only one and three times in every 10,000 births. The doctors at Loma Linda University Medical Center, a Seventh-day Adventist facility near Los Angeles, California, where Baby Fae was being treated, informed the mother, Teresa Beauclair, that there was nothing they could do to help: the child would die within a matter of days, as most babies born with HLHS did.

Despondent, Teresa took Baby Fae to a motel, where she expected to stay until her daughter died. Unemployed, without health insurance, and separated from the child's father, she seemed to have no options to help her ill baby. Then, on October 16, two days after Baby Fae was born, an unexpected ray of hope arrived when Leonard Bailey, the chief of pediatric surgery at Loma Linda, returned from a conference. Dr. Bailey contacted Teresa to propose a radical surgery that he hoped would save the child's life. Teresa and the child's father listened to Dr. Bailey's proposal and, agreeing to the terms, signed the consent forms.

Twelve days after her birth, Baby Fae underwent heart transplant surgery. The surgery was unusual, in that the new heart wasn't from another human being, but from a nine-month-old female baboon named Goobers. Only a handful of cross-species transplants – called xenografts – had been attempted before. In 1964, for example, James Hardy gave Boyd Rush, a 68-year-old deaf man, the heart of a chimpanzee, and in 1977 Christiaan Bernard attempted two simian-to-human heart transplants. All three patients died within hours or days.

Baby Fae was the first human infant to undergo a xenograft. Ten days after the surgery, on November 5, she was doing well. On that day, Dr. Bailey boldly announced that she might live to celebrate her twentieth birthday. He also predicted a future in which colonies of baboons would be raised for the purpose of donating their organs. But Dr. Bailey's optimism proved unwarranted. A few days later, Baby Fae showed the initial signs that her body was rejecting the new heart, and on November 15, twenty days after the surgery, she died. An autopsy revealed that the cause of death was the incompatibility between her blood and Goobers' blood. Whereas her blood was type O, the baboon's blood was type AB. The autopsy confirmed that the transplanted heart showed mild signs of rejection.

Criticism of the xenograft was swift in coming. Why had Dr. Bailey performed a xenograft when the few previously attempted xenografts had all resulted in failure? Wouldn't it have been better to seek a human heart first, or to transfer Baby Fae to Boston or Philadelphia, where a new corrective surgery, the Norwood procedure, was available? If Dr. Bailey was going to perform a xenograft, why did he choose the heart of a baboon rather than the heart of a chimpanzee or gorilla, given that chimps and gorillas are evolutionarily more closely related to human beings than baboons are? And shouldn't Dr. Bailey at least have chosen a baboon with the same blood type that Baby Fae had?

Dr. Bailey responded to these criticisms. He admitted that he hadn't looked for a human heart, but that was because he was convinced he wouldn't find one. Infant donors are even more difficult to find than adult donors, in part because the donor must be certified brain dead, and determining whether an infant is brain dead can be difficult, as sometimes an infant that shows no brain activity comes back to life. As it turned out, a human heart became available the day Baby Fae underwent the xenograft, but the heart couldn't have been used until the necessary tests had been conducted to see whether the heart was a suitable match for Baby Fae. This would have taken several days, time that Baby Fae, in her critical condition, may not have had. In addition, in 1984, no infant heart transplant had yet been performed, so that, even if the available heart had been suitable, performing the transplant would, like the xenograft, have been highly experimental. As for the Norwood procedure, Dr. Bailey believed, from what he knew of it, that it was generally unsuccessful, and the consent documents that Baby Fae's parents signed indicated as much. Based on these conclusions, and based on the results of the transplants he had performed in more than 150 animals over the past seven years, he believed that the xenograft he performed on Baby Fae was a reasonable option. Why did he use a baboon rather than an evolutionarily more closely related species, such as a chimpanzee or gorilla? In answer to this question, Dr. Bailey said, "Er, I find that difficult to answer. You see, I don't believe in evolution." He didn't use a baboon with the same blood type as Baby Fae because less than one percent of baboons have – and none of the seven baboons available at Loma Linda had – blood of type O, as Baby Fae had, and because he thought the immunosuppressive drugs used to prevent rejection of Goobers' heart would also take care of the problem of blood incompatibility. This decision, he confessed, was "a tactical error that came back to haunt us." He stated that, before performing any more xenografts on human beings, he would conduct more tests on animals.

Critics weren't satisfied with these answers. Dr. Bailey seemed to be uninformed about the Norwood procedure, since it had a success rate of about forty percent, much better than the zero percent success rate of prior xenografts. Also troublesome to critics was Dr. Bailey's denial of evolution, for which a wealth of evidence exists. The only real reason for using baboons, the critics maintained, was that they're easier to breed in captivity than chimpanzees or gorillas. According to the critics, Dr. Bailey seemed more interested in conducting his pet experiments than in doing what was best for Baby Fae. If this was so, perhaps the consent that Baby Fae's parents had given was tainted. Had Dr. Bailey made clear to the parents how risky the xenograft would be, and were the parents coerced into giving their consent because, lacking health insurance, they couldn't afford anything but the xenograft, which Dr. Bailey offered to perform free of charge?

Animal rights advocates, too, were upset. Picketing the Loma Linda University Medical Center, they charged that Dr. Bailey had violated Goobers' rights. In their view, even if the surgery had been successful, it would still have been morally wrong – one shouldn't sacrifice an animal, even to save a human life. Philosopher and leading animal rights advocate Tom Regan explained why. According to Regan, whether one has moral rights, including a right to life, doesn't depend on such things as how intelligent one is, whether one has the ability to use language, or whether one can understand moral concepts such as "duty" or "rights." These things are irrelevant to having moral rights because many human beings – babies and those who are severely brain-damaged, for example – lack these things but still have moral rights. Instead, Regan argues, the relevant characteristic, the characteristic one needs to have in order to have moral rights, is being a subject of a life. Subjects of a life, as Regan uses the term, are those who have some awareness of their surroundings, however minimal, and those for whom what happens to them matters to them. Human beings, including babies and the severely brain-damaged, are subjects of a life, and that's why they have moral rights. But Goobers and other animals, too, are subjects of a life. Because they can see and hear and use their other senses, they have some awareness of their surroundings, and, because they can feel pain and don't like pain, what happens to them matters to them. Thus, they, too, must have moral rights, including a right to life. Just as we should never use human beings as mere means, so we should never use animals as mere means. Regrettably, according to Regan, Goobers was used as a mere means in an effort to save Baby Fae's life.

In a commentary in the *Washington Post*, William Raspberry dismissed Regan's animal rights view out of hand: "when it comes down to a clear choice of sacrificing an animal to save a human ... the choice seems ridiculously easy. Maybe it's nothing more than my pro-human prejudice, but I don't see what all the fuss is about." Dr. Bailey took Raspberry's side: the notion of animal rights, he said, is "born of a luxurious society.... When it gets down to a human living or dying, there shouldn't be any question." Baby Fae's mother agreed. "They," she said, referring to animal rights advocates, "don't know what they're talking about."

Should Dr. Bailey have performed the xenograft on Baby Fae, or shouldn't he have? Did Dr. Bailey adequately respond to his critics, or did his critics, including the animal rights advocates, hold the stronger position? Should further research on xenografts be permitted, or should it be prohibited?

Postscript: Dr. Bailey, who died on May 12, 2019, of neck and throat cancer, never performed any more xenografts. Within a year of Baby Fae's death, he performed the world's first human-to-human infant heart transplant, and performed many more after that. Not all of his patients survived, but many are still alive and healthy. Dr. Bailey claimed that the lessons he learned from the xenograft he performed on Baby Fae helped him perform these human-to-human transplants. Thus, in his view, Baby Fae did not die in vain.

Case Study 21
A Hundred Thousand Monkeys

Throughout the first half of the twentieth century, the United States was under attack. The enemy struck ruthlessly and indiscriminately, especially during the summertime, leaving thousands dead and thousands more paralyzed. In 1952, the worst year, 3,145 Americans died and another 21,269 suffered either milder or more disabling forms of paralysis. People fought the enemy and aided the victims as best they knew how. For example, in 1927, Franklin Delano Roosevelt, who would one day become president of the United States and who himself had become a victim six years earlier and was paralyzed from the waist down, founded the Warm Springs Foundation, the first hospital devoted exclusively to the treatment of victims of this enemy. Two years later, in 1929, to help victims with severe breathing difficulties, Philip Drinker and Louis Shaw developed the iron lung. Despite such efforts, however, the battle didn't go well. Those who were lucky enough to dodge the enemy one summer knew that they, or their children, could be struck down the next summer. Everyone lived in fear.

The enemy that people in those days feared so greatly was polio. Today – thankfully – polio is no longer a threat in the United States, and it hasn't been since 1979, when the last outbreak occurred within several Amish communities. Nor is it any longer a threat in most other parts of the world. Worldwide, the number of cases of wild polio dropped from an estimated 350,000 in 1988 to a mere 1,652 in 2007, and further dropped to just 32 in 2018, all occurring in Afghanistan and Pakistan. The victory over polio, hailed as "one of the greatest events in the history of medicine," has been resounding.

Credit for the victory usually goes to Jonas Salk, who developed the first effective polio vaccine. The announcement came on April 12, 1955, on the tenth anniversary of the death of Franklin Roosevelt. Soon after the announcement, the United States initiated a massive vaccination campaign. Whereas in 1952, the year Salk began testing his vaccine, there were 57,628 reported cases of polio in the U.S., by 1961, thanks to widespread vaccinations, there were only 161 cases.

Salk, however, didn't defeat polio singlehandedly. The victory, like other medical breakthroughs, involved large numbers of researchers and took decades of hard work. In 1908 scientists discovered that polio is a virus; by the 1930s they understood that the virus comes in more than one strain, and later they determined that it comes in three strains; in 1949 they learned how to culture the virus. Without advances such as these, Salk could never have developed his vaccine. Important advances also took place after the Salk vaccine, most notably the improved vaccine developed by Albert Sabin, which after licensure in the early 1960s replaced the Salk vaccine.

All of these successes, as important as they were, make up only part of the story of the fight against polio. The other part – less frequently told, but not insignificant – consists of the failures, the missteps. Often what seemed a promising lead turned out to be a dead end. For instance, in 1935 Maurice Brodie tested what he hoped would be an effective vaccine on 3,000 children (as well as on himself and some of his assistants). Unfortunately, none of the children developed immunity to polio, and, to make matters worse, many of them had allergic reactions to the vaccine.

A complete telling of the successes and failures, the advances and missteps, would include an account, from beginning to end, of the extensive use of laboratory animals, especially monkeys. In 1908 Karl Landsteiner and Erwin Popper determined that polio is a virus when they transmitted the disease to a monkey. The ineffective vaccine that Brodie tested in 1935 used the ground-up spinal cords of monkeys. Salk cultured the polio virus in kidney cells taken from monkeys, and, before testing his vaccine on human beings, he confirmed its safety in tests on monkeys. Sabin, too, used monkeys in the development of his improved vaccine: for every sixty-five doses of vaccine produced, one monkey was killed. In the course of developing the Salk and Sabin vaccines, more than a hundred thousand monkeys were killed.

And so a moral dilemma arises. On the one hand, the end – the eradication of polio, "one of the greatest events in the history of medicine" – was noble; everyone can agree with that. But what of the means to that end? Was it morally permissible, as a means to eradicate polio, to bring suffering and death to so large a number of animals? According to defenders of animal experiments, the answer is an unequivocal yes. Although the suffering and death of a hundred thousand monkeys may, other things being equal, be a bad thing, think how many human beings worldwide would have suffered and died during the last six and a half decades had Salk and Sabin not developed their vaccines – whatever that number is, it must be far in excess of a hundred thousand. Surely, the lives and good health of that many human beings outweigh the lives and good health of a mere hundred thousand monkeys. The story of polio, say defenders of animal experiments, is proof that the use of animals in experimental procedures is necessary.

Are the defenders of animal experiments correct? Would it similarly have been justified, as a means to eradicate polio, to use a hundred thousand human beings in place of a hundred thousand monkeys? What is the difference between a hundred thousand monkeys and a hundred thousand human beings that would justify the sacrifice of the former but not of the latter?

Case Study 22
"One of the Worst Things I Had Ever Done"

Maura Anderson slipped inconspicuously into the lab, wishing that the next two hours were already behind her. A Biology major at a mid-sized university, Maura aspired to become a medical laboratory technician. Among her required courses was General Physiology, and among the requirements of General Physiology were several dissections of live frogs. During the next two hours, Maura and her classmates would be conducting the first of these dissections.

The procedure seemed simple enough. The class of twenty students would be divided into five groups of four, each group dissecting one frog. Each group would begin by pithing its frog – that is, inserting a needle into the soft portion of the frog's skull and twisting it around. This would destroy the frog's brain, rendering the frog unable to feel pain, but the frog would still be alive because respiration would continue to take place through its skin. Because it eliminates a frog's ability to feel pain, pithing is considered a humane way to dissect a live frog. Once the frog was pithed, a student would peel back the skin on the frog's legs, exposing its muscles. Then the group would use a machine – recently purchased by the Biology Department and never before used – to study contractions of the frog's gastrocnemius muscle, which is a muscle in the lower half of the leg.

Of course, the frog wouldn't survive the procedure, and this was what troubled Maura. Maura was an animal welfare advocate. A vegetarian who didn't wear leather or fur, she believed that killing frogs for the sake of a General Physiology class was unnecessary, and hence morally wrong. She considered skipping today's lab, but her professor, Marcus Delius, told the class that the lab was required and that the grade of anyone who missed it would suffer. Maura didn't want a stain on her academic record – she was an A student who regularly made the President's List – and so, reluctantly, she participated in the dissections.

Maura's misgivings gave way to outrage when the dissections went awry. The problems started when the students discovered that the frogs that the Biology Department had ordered were too small – the students couldn't find the soft portion of the frogs' skulls and so couldn't insert the needle to pith the frogs. Following Professor Delius' instructions, they resorted to an alternative method of pithing a frog, which involved taking a pair of scissors, placing one blade inside the frog's open mouth, placing the other blade behind the frog's head, and snipping off the top of the frog's head. The students were then able to insert the needle to destroy the frog's spinal cord. The frogs screamed and wriggled for roughly a minute before they finally went limp.

One of Maura's classmates, Sandy Wallace, another animal welfare advocate and a vegan, was so traumatized that she burst into tears. In response, Professor Delius said to her, "You want to become a doctor, don't you?" It was true: Sandy was a Biology major studying to become a doctor. When she continued to cry, the professor added that maybe she was trying to get into the wrong profession.

As it turned out, the frogs suffered and died in vain. When the students tried to make the frogs' muscles contract, they couldn't get the new machines to function properly, and neither could Professor Delius and his assistant. As a result, the students failed to achieve the objective of the exercise.

Several weeks later, when students who took the class were asked about the dissections, Maura said, "I can still remember the frogs crying and squirming as we cut their faces off, and how they kept moving for up to a minute later. I honestly feel that it was one of the worst things I had ever done in my life." Several other students expressed similar sentiments:

Sandy Wallace: "That was so awful!"

Chris Sanchez, who, unlike Maura and Sandy, didn't identify himself as an animal welfare advocate: "The exercise was poorly planned. The frogs were too small and the computer programs were not proven to work. Had I known this, I would have neglected taking part in such an experiment. The pain that was inflicted on the frog by pithing it through its spinal cord was terrible."

Elaine Greenwood, who also didn't think of herself as an animal welfare advocate: "The machines wouldn't work properly. Also, the frogs were too small for this lab. Because the frogs were too small, we couldn't pith the frog in an easy, humane way. Instead, the students were forced to cut the upper mouth region off the frog with scissors and then stab the frog's spinal cord.... The frog would try to kick and would whimper in pain during the process. The frogs were not treated humanely."

Tamika Sampson: "Going into this experiment, I really was excited because I do not like frogs. I think that frogs should never have existed. However, when I went into the laboratory, my whole perception changed. Seeing a live frog die right in front of my face was a first and I was terrified…. I think it was cruel because I think what I learned from killing the frog, I could have learned from watching a video on YouTube or doing something where the frogs did not have to die."

Not everyone involved with the course, however, was bothered by the dissections. One of the students, Xunli Zhang, smiled and said, "It was fun!" Professor Delius, too, supported the dissections, claiming that it would have been unethical *not* to dissect the frogs. Most of his students, he said, hope to become doctors, and doctors need to know how to cut into living tissue, as when they perform surgery on their patients. To know how to do this, they need practice. Dissecting animals in college and medical school gives them this practice. If they didn't dissect animals, their patients would suffer. To this, Professor Delius added that dissecting animals is justified because God created animals for the purpose of serving human interests. He didn't elaborate, but he may have had in mind the opening chapter of Genesis, the first book of the Bible. According to Genesis, God created the world in six days, creating human beings last of all. Unlike animals, human beings were created in God's image, and God granted human beings dominion over animals: "Then God said, 'Let us make man in our image, after our likeness; and let them have dominion over the fish of the sea, and over the birds of the air, and over the cattle, and over all the earth, and over every creeping thing that creeps upon the earth'" (Genesis 1:26).

Most of Professor Delius' colleagues in the Biology Department concurred – requiring college students majoring in Biology to dissect animals, they held, is appropriate. In fact, there was only one dissenter, Professor Arthur Sylvester, who, believing that one can be a good biologist without killing animals, never required dissections in his own classes. In his view, students at the very least should be allowed to opt out of participating in dissections – this would be the only way to respect those who have moral objections. Disturbed by what had happened in Professor Delius' class, Professor Sylvester looked into what the law said about dissections. He found a law that had recently been passed stating that students must be allowed to opt out without penalty – but this law applied only to high school students, not college students. Everything Professor Delius had done was within the law.

Should dissections of animals be required in college biology classes, or should they be optional – or abandoned altogether? What changes, if any, should Professor Delius make the next time he teaches General Physiology?

Postscript: The dissections that were required of Maura Anderson and her classmates took place in the Spring 2013 semester. A year later, in Spring 2014, Professor Delius once again taught General Physiology and once again required his students to carry out dissections. This time, the frogs were the right size and the equipment functioned properly. Nonetheless, one of the students, Jennifer Saunders, an ardent animal lover, objected. She borrowed from an animal rights organization a sophisticated computer program for conducting simulated dissections. She asked Professor Delius if he would take a look at the program and allow her to use it rather than participate in a real dissection. She assured him that she had no aspirations of becoming a doctor but instead was studying to become a medical laboratory technician. As a medical laboratory technician, she wouldn't perform any surgeries and hence wouldn't need practice cutting into living tissue. She also asked Professor Delius if he would take a look at a peer-reviewed scientific article showing that students who conduct simulated dissections perform on exams as well as, or even better than, students who conduct real dissections. Professor Delius declined to look at any of the materials Jennifer had brought for him and reaffirmed that, if she didn't participate in the dissections, her course grade would be adversely affected. After weighing her options, Jennifer chose to skip all the labs in which dissections took place. She was a straight A student – except for General Physiology. In that course, she received a C.

In Spring 2015, the next time he taught General Physiology, Professor Delius had his assistant perform all dissections. The students in the class merely observed. In 2016, the last medical school in the United States or Canada to use live animals to teach surgery – the University of Tennessee College of Medicine in Chattanooga – announced that it would cease the practice. According to the Physicians Committee for Responsible Medicine, the practice "is not essential," as lifelike simulators of human bodies are now available.

Part 4
THE AMERICAN HEALTH CARE SYSTEM

Case Study 23
A Hopelessly Flawed System?

Tom Adams had had stomach problems for most of his life. The pain would strike once or twice a month, usually in the evening after dinner, and it would often last several hours. Adams had always assumed that it was only gas, and so he'd never bothered to see a doctor. But now, as he was approaching his forty-fifth birthday, his stomach was taking a turn for the worse. He felt pain almost every day, and the pain could come any time of day, not just the evening. Sometimes eating seemed to help, but other times it seemed to make the pain worse. Gas-X, Tums, and other over-the-counter medications proved ineffective. The pain made sleeping difficult, and – most troubling of all – Adams was losing weight, ten pounds in the last several weeks. He decided it was time to see a doctor.

Adams only rarely saw a doctor. This wasn't because he had anything against doctors. On the contrary, he knew that many doctors genuinely cared about their patients. No, the real problem, he thought, was the system – the American health care system. It seemed to him that the system was more about making money than keeping people healthy. There was – to take just one of many instances – the pharmaceutical industry. Worldwide, the pharmaceutical industry was more than a half trillion dollar a year industry. Nearly half of that vast sum of money came from the United States. Did people really need to ingest so many pharmaceuticals? Adams had doubts.

So Adams didn't really want to see a doctor. But under the circumstances, he didn't know what else to do. After flipping through the Yellow Pages and doing a little research on the Internet, Adams called a gastroenterology center in town. The woman on the other end of the line told him that the earliest appointment she could give him was three weeks away. He was disappointed that he'd have to wait that long, but he thought he'd be able to make it, and thus he took the appointment. In the meantime, he didn't eat any oily or spicy foods, hoping that would help, and he kept what he called a "stomach log": every day he wrote down everything he ate, and every day he wrote down whether he experienced pain and when he experienced it. Luckily, the pain soon eased up.

On January 19, 2007, Adams arrived at the gastroenterology center, fifteen minutes early for his 9:30 appointment. After filling out some paperwork, he sat in the waiting room until 10:00, when someone led him into a second waiting room. He sat down on a plush sofa there, feeling a little ill at ease. Despite the comfortable furniture and the artwork adorning the walls, the room felt impersonal and antiseptic. Adams preferred the familiar clutter of his own home. Then, just before 10:30, he was led into an examination room. Once there, he waited another ten minutes.

Finally, a young woman entered the examination room, dressed in a white lab coat. She introduced herself, telling Adams that she was a graduate student at a nearby university studying to become a Physician's Assistant. She would be conducting the initial examination. She began by asking Adams several questions. When he told her that he didn't have a primary care physician, she said, "Why not?" Her voice was faintly accusatory. "If I have a problem, I go directly to a specialist," Adams replied. He didn't like her faintly accusatory voice, so he didn't elaborate. He didn't tell her that he saw no point having a primary care physician. A primary care physician would only refer him to a specialist, and then he'd have to pay two bills instead of one. He had a hard enough time making ends meet as it was. He couldn't afford to throw money out the window.

The woman asked Adams to lie down on the examination table. With her fingers, she pressed against his stomach, one part of it after another, each time asking him whether it hurt. Almost every time he answered yes, but it especially hurt when she pressed just below his breastbone. When she finished her examination, he gave her the "stomach log" he'd been keeping and she left the room.

A few minutes later, she returned with the doctor and a nurse. The doctor – a middle-aged man with a bit of a paunch – praised Adams for keeping the "stomach log," and told him that he wanted him to take a series of tests: a blood test, an ultrasound, an MRI, and an endoscopy. As he spoke, the doctor exuded such confidence that Adams, despite having a skeptical nature, found himself trusting the doctor implicitly. When the doctor was finished – the conversation couldn't have lasted five minutes – he asked if Adams had any questions, and when Adams shook his head no, the doctor left the room. Only later, after he'd had time to mull on it, did Adams realize that, in fact, he had several questions for the doctor. He was surprised that the doctor didn't ask him about his diet, such as whether the foods he listed in his "stomach log" were foods he typically ate, and he was surprised that the doctor didn't ask him about his lifestyle. Did he, for example, exercise regularly, and was his job stressful? Why didn't the doctor want to know about such things? Perhaps they weren't relevant?

The nurse – also middle-aged with a bit of a paunch – gave Adams several packets of pills. She said he should take them in case he had an ulcer. Adams didn't like taking pills, and he was surprised that the nurse gave him pills before the doctor had reached a diagnosis. He decided, however, to give them a try. When he got home, he opened a packet and took out a purple gel cap. "Why do they have to be so big?" he muttered to himself. Once, many years ago, he had tried to swallow a pill. He placed it on the back of his tongue and took a drink of water, but the pill stubbornly refused to go down. He tried several times, with the same result. Eventually, he gave up.

Adams didn't even attempt to swallow the purple gel gap. Instead, he carefully unscrewed it, and peered at the contents inside – tiny white beads, like the sugar candy on top of a nonpareil. He was willing to bet, though, that the tiny white beads didn't taste like sugar. Bracing himself, he dumped the contents of the gel cap into his mouth, took a drink of water, avoided crushing the beads with his teeth as much he could, and swallowed. But the tiny white beads weren't bitter! If anything, they were slightly sweet. Puzzled, Adams looked again at the packet of gel caps. Could they be placebos? Why would the nurse give him placebos? Did she and the doctor suspect that his pain was all in his mind? Adams shook his head, but he continued to take the pills. A few weeks later, when he'd taken them all, his stomach was no better.

On the same day that he visited the gastroenterology center – January 19 – Adams went to Quest Diagnostics for his blood test. On January 23 he had the ultrasound, on February 9 the MRI, and on February 16 the endoscopy. None of the procedures was painful, though for the endoscopy he was placed under general anesthesia. Adams liked the anesthesiologist. The fellow was friendly, and he took the time to explain to Adams what to expect – for example, that, even after he woke up from the procedure, Adams would be sleepy for the rest of the day.

The battery of tests that Adams took revealed very little. He evidently had a varicose vein on his liver, though the doctor thought that had nothing to do with the pain he was experiencing. In addition, as the endoscopy showed, his stomach was slightly red. But that was all. At least Adams knew he didn't have an ulcer, and he knew he didn't have cancer. He also didn't have gastroesophageal reflux disease (GERD), a hiatal hernia (protrusion of the stomach into the diaphragm), or a Schatzki ring (a narrowing of the esophagus). The tests ruled those out. But he still didn't know what was wrong with him.

Then the bills started pouring in: $250 for the initial office visit; about the same for the blood test; $200 for the ultrasound; $1,300 for the MRI; $1,800 for the endoscopy. Adams muttered under his breath as he thought about his health insurance. Just five years ago, he still hadn't had any insurance. Going without insurance had made him nervous, but he'd only had part-time work and on his meager salary he couldn't afford insurance. Then he landed a full-time position. For the first time in his life, he purchased health insurance. The insurance agent explained to him about deductibles. The higher the deductible, the lower his premiums would be. Adams wasn't sure which deductible to choose. In the end, since he only rarely saw a doctor, he opted for a high deductible: $5,000. The bills he was now receiving totaled not quite $4,000. He'd be paying the whole thing from his own pocket. He wondered if all those tests he took were really necessary. All they did was to take his money; they did nothing for his stomach.

Adams' doctor wanted Adams to make another appointment with him. The appointment would have to be next Wednesday at 2:30 in the afternoon, the only time that week that the doctor was available. Adams would have to take time off from work. He didn't like missing work – in the last two decades, he hadn't missed even a day. He had never been seriously ill, and he'd always managed to make necessary appointments either on Fridays, when he didn't work, or early in the morning, before he had to leave for work. He debated whether he should take the appointment. The doctor, it seemed by now, wouldn't be able to help Adams' stomach; probably he'd want to talk only about the varicose vein on Adams' liver. In the end, though, Adams took the appointment. He'd give the doctor one more chance to help him.

Adams left work early that Wednesday. He got caught in traffic – another highway accident – but he still arrived just in time for his appointment. He ran into the office, out of breath, and told the receptionist he had a 2:30 appointment with the doctor. The receptionist knitted her brows, looked through her appointment book, and then said, "I'm sorry. Your appointment was for 1:30. The doctor has already left." Adams tried to explain that his appointment was for 2:30, not 1:30, but the receptionist's appointment book clearly had him down for 1:30. The receptionist said that probably *he* was the one who'd made a mistake. "Would you like to schedule another appointment?" she asked.

Adams sat down on a nearby bench and buried his face in his hands. He sat on the bench for a long time. He was angry, and the longer he sat on the bench the angrier he became. He was angry for many reasons. He didn't like the long wait to see the doctor; he didn't like how little time the doctor spent with him; he didn't like the university student's faintly accusatory voice; he didn't like taking pills; he didn't like taking so many tests with so little result; he didn't like the insurance industry; he didn't like leaving work early and battling traffic only to be told that he'd missed his appointment and that it was all his fault.

At length, he got up and strode out of the office. As the door slammed shut behind him, he muttered under his breath, "Hopeless! The whole system is hopelessly flawed!"

Adams' experience at the gastroenterology center didn't go well. Could the medical personnel Adams dealt with have handled things better? Could Adams have handled things better? Was Adams right: is something wrong with the American health care system? If so, what precisely is wrong with it, and what can be done to make it better?

Postscript: In the last dozen years, Adams' stomach problems have persisted, though he's gained back the ten pounds that he'd lost. In 2013 and 2014 he kept another "stomach log." The log of 2013 shows that his stomach gave him problems on thirty-seven days during the year, while the log of 2014 shows that his stomach gave him problems on twenty days. In 2015 he again saw a gastroenterologist, but a different one. He had picked up a copy of his records from his previous gastroenterologist to show the new gastroenterologist. Shuffling through the records, the new gastroenterologist stated that the MRI Adams had taken was unnecessary and that the results of the endoscopy from eight years earlier were unhelpful. To Adams' surprise, the records asserted that

- the ulcer pills Adams had been given were Prevacid, not a placebo;
- the varicose vein on Adams' liver was in fact a hemangioma, a benign growth that likely disappeared after its discovery in 2007 and was no cause for worry;

- Adams had had stomach problems for only six months, when in fact he had had stomach problems for most of his life;
- Adams was eating a traditional American diet, even though the foods listed in his "stomach log," the only information the doctor had had about his diet, were all vegetarian. In fact, in 2007, when he gave the doctor his stomach log, Adams had been a vegetarian for fifteen years.

Adams' new doctor recommended an endoscopy, but no other tests. The endoscopy showed that Adams had GERD, a hiatal hernia, and a Schatzki ring – all of which his previous endoscopy showed he didn't have. The doctor told Adams that over-the-counter omeprazole, an acid-reducing drug, should help, as should abstaining from acid-producing foods such as tomatoes, onions, oranges, and chocolate. Adams did as the doctor suggested, but noticed no improvement. At least, though, the endoscopy cost Adams only $30, because a few years earlier he had purchased new health insurance through his employer, which requires copays rather than deductibles.

Case Study 24
Obamacare

On March 23, 2010, President Barack Obama signed into law the Patient Protection and Affordable Care Act (ACA), the most significant health care reform in the U.S. since the introduction of Medicare and Medicaid in 1965. From the outset, the ACA – popularly known as Obamacare – was highly controversial. Not a single Republican in either the House or the Senate voted for it, and all the while Obama was president Republican lawmakers voted repeatedly to repeal the law – only to see the president veto the repeals. Soon after the ACA was enacted, twenty-eight of the fifty states filed lawsuits to overturn several of its key provisions. Eventually, the lawsuits reached the U.S. Supreme Court, which in 2012 upheld most of the ACA, but only by a bare 5-4 majority. In 2015 the ACA was once again before the Supreme Court, and once again the Court came to its rescue, this time by a vote of 6-3. When Donald Trump became president, he vowed that he and the Republican-controlled Congress would quickly repeal and replace the ACA, but the process proved more difficult than Trump anticipated. On July 28, 2017, six months into the Trump presidency, the Senate cast another vote on health care, falling short of a partial repeal of the ACA by one vote – although near the end of 2017 Congress managed to eliminate one of the ACA's key provisions, namely the mandate that nearly all Americans purchase health insurance. While its future continues to be uncertain, the bulk of the ACA – for better or worse – remains the law of the land.

The purpose of the ACA was to avert a growing crisis in the American health care system. Fueling the crisis were (1) skyrocketing health care costs and (2) limited access to health care.

1. Costs

In 2010, the year the ACA was enacted but before most of its provisions took effect, the United States spent in excess of $2.5 trillion on health care. That represented 17.6 percent of America's gross domestic product (GDP) and $8,233 for every man, woman, and child in the country. The U.S. spent more on health care in 2010 than did any other country in the world, and it spent more in 2010 than it had in any previous year. Canada, for example, spent only $4,445 per person in 2010, which amounted to 11.4 percent of its GDP. And in 1970 the U.S. spent just $75 billion on health care, about 7 percent of its GDP.

Many factors contributed to the high cost of American health care. Here are a few of the most salient ones:

An aging population. As the baby boom generation has grown older, the median age of the population in the U.S. has increased. Older people need more, and more costly, health care than do younger people.

Pharmaceuticals. In 1990 Americans spent $40 billion on drugs; in 2006 they spent $217 billion. According to pharmaceutical companies, the costs of research and development account for this increase. Critics, by contrast, argue that pharmaceutical companies often produce and market new drugs that are more expensive but no more effective than drugs that are already available. A frequently cited example was the marketing of Nexium, a drug for stomach acid, after the patent for Prilosec expired in 2001. From 2001 to 2005, Nexium netted its manufacturer, AstraZeneca, $39 billion. Nexium's chemical makeup is similar to Prilosec's, and critics have charged that the effectiveness of the two drugs is about the same.

New technology. Over the years, the U.S. has developed new medical technology and made it widely available. Examples include the technology of CT scans and MRIs. New technology, however, tends to be more costly than older technology.

Administrative costs. At the time the ACA was enacted, most U.S. citizens paid for their health care through insurance companies. Insurance companies must create and market benefits packages, decide whom they will cover, set premiums, and review and either accept or reject claims. All this carries with it large administrative costs. By contrast, Canadians have a single-payer system, in which everyone is provided with a basic package of benefits, and the government, through taxes, pays for it. (If they want, Canadians can purchase more extensive coverage from private insurance companies.) The Canadian government doesn't need to decide whom to cover, since everyone is covered, and it doesn't need to do as much of the other administrative work that U.S. insurance companies do. The upshot is that, at the time the ACA was enacted, U.S. citizens paid $752 per person per year more in administrative costs than did Canadians. This is one instance in which more government meant less bureaucracy.

2. Access

Although Americans spent more on health care in 2010 than did any other nation in the world, Americans were arguably not the world's healthiest people. According to United Nations statistics, during the years 2005-2010, the United States ranked only fortieth among 192 nations in terms of life expectancy (78.20 years), and only fortieth among 182 nations in terms of infant mortality (7 deaths per 1,000 live births). By contrast, Canada – ranked eleventh and thirty-third, respectively – had a life expectancy of 80.77 years and an infant mortality of 5 deaths per 1,000 live births. Japan had the highest life expectancy in the world at 82.66 years, and Singapore had the lowest infant mortality at 2 deaths per 1,000 live births.

One of the reasons the United States fared less well than some other countries was that, as health care costs rose, many Americans found purchasing insurance increasingly difficult. In 2010, an estimated thirty-seven million to forty-five million Americans (12-15 percent of the population) had no health insurance. Perhaps an additional fifteen million went without insurance for a portion of the year, as they left one job and moved on to another. Uninsured Americans fell into a number of categories:

- People whom insurance companies denied coverage because they had a preexisting condition – for example, they had HIV or had at some time in the past been treated for breast cancer.
- People whom insurance companies stopped covering because they had exceeded their lifetime coverage cap. Insurance companies often paid out only so much to a policyholder – perhaps a million dollars – during the policyholder's lifetime. Policyholders who had expensive illnesses that required repeated treatments sometimes exceeded their lifetime coverage cap – and lost their insurance.
- People who were unemployed and couldn't afford insurance.
- People whose employers didn't provide insurance and who couldn't afford their own insurance.
- People whose employers provided insurance, but only if their employees paid a portion of the premiums. Some people couldn't afford to pay their portion of the premiums.
- The spouses or children of people whose employers provided insurance only for their employees, not their employees'

families. Children made up about a quarter of all uninsured Americans.
- People who could afford insurance but, for whatever reason, chose not to purchase it.

Provisions of the ACA

The ACA handles the problems of cost and access in the following ways:

Starting in 2014, aside from a few exceptions, all Americans were required to purchase health insurance. The exceptions included Native Americans, those who objected to insurance for religious reasons, and those whose incomes were low enough that they didn't need to file an income tax return. Anyone else who failed to purchase health insurance had to pay a fee. In 2016, the fee was 2.5 percent of the person's annual income, or $695 if that was higher. This mandate to purchase health insurance was the provision that, near the end of 2017, the Republican-controlled Congress eliminated.

Those with an income less than 133 percent of the poverty level ($14,400 for an individual and $29,327 for a family of four) qualify for insurance through Medicaid, a government-run health care program for poorer Americans. According to the 2012 Supreme Court ruling, however, states can, if they wish, opt out of this provision of the ACA. Nearly three quarters of states have opted out.

Most Americans continue to get their health insurance through their employers. Those who are self-employed, or don't need to work, or aren't poor enough to get insurance through Medicaid are able to purchase health insurance from an insurance exchange. Insurance exchanges are set up by the states. The United States has not adopted a Canadian-style single-payer system.

During the years 2010-2013, small businesses received tax credits if they provided health insurance for their employees. If a small business paid half of its employees' premiums, it recovered in the form of a tax credit seventy percent of what it paid. In effect, then, it paid only fifteen percent of its employees' premiums.

Starting in 2014, insurance companies were no longer permitted to deny coverage to those who have a preexisting condition. Nor were they permitted to place a cap on lifetime benefits. If a policyholder accumulates millions of dollars in medical expenses, the insurance company has to pay.

Starting in September 2010, insurance companies were required to cover preventive care at no additional cost. Preventive care includes, for example, HIV tests, mammograms, and flu shots. The rationale for this provision of the ACA was to save money: preventing an illness, or curing an illness when it's at an early stage, tends to be less expensive than tackling an illness at an advanced stage. It should be noted, however, that this provision of the ACA applied only to new policyholders. Those who already held a policy didn't likely receive coverage for preventive care.

Starting in 2011, Medicare, a government-run health care program for people aged sixty-five and older, was required to cover preventive care, just as private insurance companies were the year before. Starting in 2013, people with annual incomes in excess of $200,000 saw an increase in their payroll tax contributions to Medicare. The contribution increased from 1.45 percent to 2.35 percent.

Evaluation of the ACA

Just about everyone agrees that the U.S. health care system needed an overhaul. Whether the ACA was the right kind of overhaul, however, remains a matter of intense dispute. Critics of the ACA are divided into two camps.

One group of critics argues that the ACA goes too far. The founding fathers of the United States valued the freedom of the individual. The proper role of government, they thought, was to protect individual liberty. Anything beyond that was going too far. The ACA, however, goes beyond protecting individual liberty. In fact, it encroaches on individual liberty. Under the ACA – before the Republican-controlled Congress abolished the provision in 2017 – individuals were no longer free to decline health insurance. They had to purchase insurance, or lose 2.5% of their income. Under the ACA, owners of insurance companies are no longer free to run their businesses as they see fit. They must cover people with preexisting conditions, they can't put a cap on lifetime benefits, and they must cover preventive care. However beneficial these things may be, they interfere with individual liberty. They are a violation of basic rights. Such things, according to the first group of critics, should never be permitted.

The second group of critics argues that the ACA doesn't go far enough. The problem with the ACA, according to these critics, isn't that it involves too much government. The problem is that it involves too little government. The second group of critics favors a Canadian-style single-payer system. As long as the U.S. continues to rely so heavily on insurance companies, administrative costs will continue to be high, and as long as administrative costs continue to be high, many people will continue to have a hard time affording quality health insurance. The health of Americans will continue to lag behind the health of people elsewhere in the world. Perhaps the ACA is better than things used to be, but the United States could do even better than the ACA.

Is the ACA really better than things used to be? Can the United States really do better than the ACA? Data gathered since the enactment of the ACA suggest that the answer to both questions may be "Yes." Since 2010, the cost of health care in the U.S. has continued to increase – from $2.5 trillion ($8,233 for every man, woman, and child in the country) to $3.3 trillion in 2016 ($10,348 for every man, woman, and child in the country). Better news for the ACA is that many more Americans acquired health insurance under it than they did before it. For example, whereas in 2017 only 8.8 percent of Americans were uninsured, in 2013, the last year Americans could decline health insurance without penalty, 13.3 percent of Americans were uninsured. (Now that the mandate to purchase health insurance has been repealed, the number of uninsured Americans may once again increase.) This achievement of the ACA, however, is still a far cry from the universal coverage that a single-payer system like Canada's provides. Canadians believe that everyone has a right to a decent minimum of health care. If Americans were to adopt this belief, perhaps their health would improve.

So who is right? Does the ACA go too far? Does it not go far enough? Or is it an appropriate response to the problems of high health care costs and limited access to health care?

SOURCES AND FURTHER READING

Case Study 1: Obesity

American Diabetes Association. (2018). Economic costs of diabetes in the U.S. in 2017. Retrieved from https://care.diabetesjournals.org/content/early/2018/03/20/dci18-0007

Bottemiller Evich, H. (May 7, 2018). Obama's calorie rule kicks in thanks to Trump. *Politico*. Retrieved from https://www.politico.com/story/2018/05/07/fdacalories-food-labels-obama-trump-517191

Eckholm, E. (December 1, 2006). Medicaid plan prods patients toward health. *The New York Times*. Retrieved from https://www.nytimes.com/2006/12/01/us/01medicaid.html

Hales, C. M., Carroll, M. D., Fryar, C. D., & Ogden, C. L. (2017). Prevalence of obesity among adults and youth: United States, 2015-2016. NCHS Data Brief, No. 288. Retrieved from https://www.cdc.gov/nchs/data/databriefs/db288.pdf

Hospers, J. (1971). *Libertarianism: A political philosophy for tomorrow*. Nash.

Jones, M., Huffer, C., Adams, T., Jones, L., & Church, B. (2018). BMI health report cards: Parents' perceptions and reactions. Retrieved from https://www.ncbi.nlm.nih.gov/pubmed/29388480

NetCE. (December 1, 2017). Childhood obesity: Impact on health care. Retrieved from https://www.netce.com/casestudies.php?courseid=1565

Tsai, A. G., Williamson, D. F., & Glick, H. A. (2011). Direct medical cost of overweight and obesity in the United States: A quantitative systematic review. Retrieved from https://www.ncbi.nlm.nih.gov/pmc/articles/PMC2891924/

Case Study 2: Barbie

American Society of Plastic Surgeons. (2019). 2018 plastic surgery statistics report. Retrieved from https://www.plasticsurgery.org/documents/News/Statistics/2018/plastic-surgery-statistics-full-report-2018.pdf

Dolgin, E. (December 4, 2015). Plastic surgeons, fearing violence, turn to psychiatry to screen patients. *STAT*. Retrieved from https://www.statnews.com/2015/12/04/plastic-surgeons-psychiatry-screening/

Mill, J. S. *Utilitarianism*. Any edition.

Peppers, M. (July 25, 2013). "It's hard not being in control of my body": Plastic surgery addict who has had 59 procedures on being forced to accept her looks after sudden weight gain. *Daily Mail*. Retrieved from http://www.dailymail.co.uk/femail/article-2378117/Plastic-surgery-addict-Jenny-Lee-forced-accept-looks-sudden-weight-gain.html

Case Study 3: "Please Let Me Die"

Cowart, D. (2012). Dax Cowart – 40 years later. Retrieved from https://vimeo.com/channels/1045234/64585949

Cowart, D., & Burt, R. (1998). Confronting death: Who chooses, who controls? A dialogue between Dax Cowart and Robert Burt. Retrieved from https://pdfs.semanticscholar.org/d3f8/93a0f593b884714fc88dcb68e5d6b55d3f3a.pdf?_ga=2.53067048.1837327209.1563286054-1380577161.1563286054

Kant, I. *Groundwork for the metaphysics of morals*. Any edition.

Steinbach, A. (April 26, 1998). "Please let me die." *The Baltimore Sun*. Retrieved from https://www.baltimoresun.com/news/bs-xpm-1998-04-26-1998116064-story.html

Steinbach, A. (April 27, 1998). "Let me fix your hands. And then ... you can kill yourself." *The Baltimore Sun*. Retrieved from https://www.baltimoresun.com/news/bs-xpm-1998-04-27-1998117064-story.html

Steinbach, A. (April 28, 1998). "I've given it everything. I don't think I can make my life work." *The Baltimore Sun*. Retrieved from https://www.baltimoresun.com/news/bs-xpm-1998-04-28-1998118140-story.html

Case Study 4: "I Don't Want It Done"

Annas, G. J. (1988). She's going to die: The case of Angela C. *The Hastings Center Report, 18*(1), 23-25.

District of Columbia Court of Appeals. (November 10, 1987). *In re: AC*. Retrieved from https://law.justia.com/cases/district-of-columbia/court-of-appeals/1987/87-609-0-0.html

Gellman, B. (April 27, 1990). Mother's right upheld over fetus's. *The Washington Post*. Retrieved from https://www.washingtonpost.com/archive/politics/1990/04/27/mothers-right-upheld-over-fetuss/b5b76521-b21a-46ab-b300-a4a9bb6280ff/?utm_term=.97e2be8e591d

Greenhouse, L. (April 27, 1990). Court in capital bars forced surgery to save fetus. *The New York Times*. Retrieved from https://www.nytimes.com/1990/04/27/us/court-in-capital-bars-forced-surgery-to-save-fetus.html

Case Study 5: The *Tarasoff* Decision

Ewing, C. P., & McCann, J. T. (2006). Prosenjit Poddar and Tatiana Tarasoff: Where the public peril begins. In *Minds on trial: Great cases in law and psychology*, pp. 57-68. Oxford University Press.

Supreme Court of California. (July 1, 1976). *Tarasoff v. Regents of University of California*. Retrieved from https://law.justia.com/cases/california/supreme-court/3d/17/425.html

Case Study 6: Noble Lies

Bok, Sissela. (1999). *Lying: Moral choice in public and private life*. Vintage.

Kant, I. On a supposed right to lie because of philanthropic concerns. Any edition.

MacFarquhar, L. (October 1, 2018). The comforting fictions of dementia care. *The New Yorker*. Retrieved from https://www.newyorker.com/magazine/2018/10/08/the-comforting-fictions-of-dementia-care

Plato. *Republic*. Any edition.

Case Study 7: Jack Kevorkian

Biography.com Editors. (April 2, 2014, last updated April 17, 2019). Jack Kevorkian biography. Retrieved from https://www.biography.com/scientist/jack-kevorkian

Kevorkian, J., & Wallace, M. (November 22, 1998). Death by doctor. *60 Minutes*. Retrieved from https://www.cbsnews.com/video/death-by-doctor/

Case Study 8: Terri Schiavo

Caplan, A. L., McCartney, J. J., & Sisti, D. A. (eds.). (2006). *The case of Terri Schiavo: Ethics at the end of life*. Prometheus.

Cermenara, K., & Goodman, K. (July 28, 2005). Key events in the case of Theresa Marie Schiavo. Retrieved from http://science.jburroughs.org/mbahe/BioEthics/Articles/SchiavoTimeline.pdf

Case Study 9: Miss Sherri
Anonymous. (August 19, 1962). Mrs. Finkbine undergoes abortion in Sweden; surgeon asserts unborn child was deformed – mother of 4 took thalidomide. *The New York Times*. Retrieved from https://www.nytimes.com/1962/08/19/archives/mrs-finkbine-undergoes-abortion-in-sweden-surgeon-asserts-unborn.html?sq=finkbine&scp=40&st=p

Planned Parenthood Advocates of Arizona. (August 15, 2012). Sherri Finkbine's abortion: Its meaning 50 years later. Retrieved from http://advocatesaz.org/2012/08/15/sherri-finkbines-abortion-its-meaning-50-years-later/

Singer, P. (2011). *Practical ethics*, 3rd ed. Cambridge University Press. See especially pp. 160-167.

Case Study 10: *Roe v. Wade*
McCorvey, N., & Thomas, G. (1997). *Won by love*. Thomas Nelson, Inc.

Prager, J. (December 28, 2017). Norma McCorvey: The woman who became Roe – and then regretted it. *Politico*. Retrieved from https://www.politico.com/magazine/story/2017/12/28/norma-mccorvey-obituary-216184

United States Supreme Court. (January 22, 1973). *Roe v. Wade*. Retrieved from https://caselaw.findlaw.com/us-supreme-court/410/113.html

Case Study 11: The Octomom
Anonymous. (January 31, 2009). Octuplets' mom "obsessed" with having kids. *CBS News*. Retrieved from https://www.cbsnews.com/news/octuplets-mom-obsessed-with-having-kids/

Anonymous. (March 3, 2009). Octuplet mom's ex: We split because we couldn't have kids. *Us Magazine*. Retrieved from https://web.archive.org/web/20090304190701/http://www.usmagazine.com/news/octo-moms-ex-we-split-because-we-couldnt-have-kids-200933

Curry, A. (February 10, 2009). Her side of the story: Nadya Suleman shares details about her family, which now includes 14 kids. *Dateline NBC*. Retrieved from http://www.nbcnews.com/id/29129311/ns/dateline_nbc-newsmakers/t/her-side-story/#.XS8mH-hKiM9

Rocha, V. (July 14, 2014). "Octomom" pleads no contest to welfare fraud, gets community service. *Los Angeles Times*. Retrieved from https://www.latimes.com/local/lanow/la-me-ln-octomom-pleads-no-contest-welfare-fraud-20140714-story.html

Rubin, R. (October 18, 2009). "Octomom" doctor expelled from fertility group. *USA Today*. Retrieved from https://usatoday30.usatoday.com/news/health/2009-10-18-octomom-doctor-fertility_N.htm

Yoshino, K., & Garrison, J. (February 11, 2009). Octuplets could be costly for taxpayers. *Los Angeles Times*. Retrieved from https://web.archive.org/web/20090318110016/http://www.latimes.com/news/local/la-me-octuplets11-2009feb11,0,1790195.story

Case Study 12: Baby M

Baby M Surrogacy Contract. (February 6, 1985). Retrieved from https://www.ericgoldman.org/contracts/babymcontracts.htm

Superior Court of New Jersey, Chancery Division Family Part, Bergen County. (March 31, 1987). *In Re Baby M*. Retrieved from https://law.justia.com/cases/new-jersey/appellate-division-published/1987/217-n-j-super-313-0.html

Supreme Court of New Jersey. (February 3, 1988). *In the matter of Baby M*. Retrieved from https://law.justia.com/cases/new-jersey/supreme-court/1988/109-n-j-396-1.html

Case Study 13: Savior Sibling

Mohyeldin, A. (May 22, 2013). Born to save her sister's life, Marissa Ayala graduates from college. *NBC Nightly News*. Retrieved from https://www.nbcnews.com/nightly-news/video/born-to-save-her-sisters-life-marissa-ayala-graduates-from-college-31121987902

Morrow, L. (June 17, 1991). When one body can save another. *Time Magazine, 137*(24).

Case Study 14: Autism and Vaccination

Berman, M. (April 16, 2014). Jenny McCarthy says she isn't anti-vaccine. Here are some other things she has said about vaccinations.

The Washington Post. Retrieved from https://www.washingtonpost.com/news/post-nation/wp/2014/04/16/jenny-mccarthy-says-she-isnt-anti-vaccine-here-are-some-other-things-she-has-said-about-vaccinations/?noredirect=on&utm_term=.4f0d94686dac

Chabris, C., & Simons, D. (2011). *The invisible gorilla: How our intuitions deceive us* (pp. 174-183). Harmony.

Eggertson, L. (March 9, 2010). *Lancet* retracts 12-year-old article linking autism to MMR vaccines. *Canadian Medical Association Journal, 182*(4), E199-E200. Retrieved from https://www.ncbi.nlm.nih.gov/pmc/articles/PMC2831678/

National Conference of State Legislatures. (June 14, 2019). States with religious and philosophical exemptions from school immunization requirements. Retrieved from http://www.ncsl.org/research/health/school-immunization-exemption-state-laws.aspx

Case Study 15: Christian Science versus Medical Science

Anonymous. (July 5, 1990). Boston jury convicts 2 Christian Scientists in death of a son. *The New York Times*. Retrieved from https://www.nytimes.com/1990/07/05/us/boston-jury-convicts-2-christian-scientists-in-death-of-a-son.html

Daly, C. B. (July 3, 1990). Trial on death of toddler, faith healing goes to jury. *The Washington Post*. Retrieved from https://www.washingtonpost.com/archive/politics/1990/07/03/trial-on-death-of-toddler-faith-healing-goes-to-jury/3c552061-5b17-4d73-b4fa-d3dba11d923d/?utm_term=.141a4f0ddba2

Daly, C. B. (July 5, 1990). Parents who relied on faith healing are convicted in son's death. *The Washington Post*. Retrieved from https://www.washingtonpost.com/archive/politics/1990/07/05/parents-who-relied-on-faith-healing-are-convicted-in-sons-death/efbcd5eb-e0ab-437e-91c0-8d6f2e7f99de/?noredirect=on&utm_term=.e3815606b6d3

Margolick, D. (August 6, 1990). In child's death, a test for Christian Science. *The New York Times*. Retrieved from https://www.nytimes.com/1990/08/06/us/in-child-deaths-a-test-for-christian-science.html?mtrref=www.google.com&gwh=A377C0081156E26D8E77E607B024EB0D&gwt=pay

Massachusetts Supreme Judicial Court. (August 11, 1993). *Commonwealth v. Twitchell*. Retrieved from https://www.courtlistener.com/opinion/2040533/commonwealth-v-twitchell/

Case Study 16: The Vegan Baby
Kilgannon, C. (March 26, 2003). Trial underway in case of vegetarians' sick child. *The New York Times*. Retrieved from https://www.nytimes.com/2003/03/26/nyregion/trial-under-way-in-case-of-vegetarians-sick-child.html
Mangan, D. (March 26, 2003). Doc boosts vegan duo – don't blame diet for baby's withered state, he testifies. *New York Post*. Retrieved from https://nypost.com/2003/03/26/doc-boosts-vegan-duo-dont-blame-diet-for-babys-withered-state-he-testifies/
Mangan, D. (April 1, 2003). Mom: Kid "thrived" on vegan diet. *New York Post*. Retrieved from https://nypost.com/2003/04/01/mom-kid-thrived-on-vegan-diet/
New York Appellate Division, Second Department. (November 16, 2005). *People v. Swinton*. Retrieved from http://courts.state.ny.us/Reporter/3dseries/2005/2005_06814.htm
Retsinas, G. (April 5, 2003). Couple guilty of assault in vegan case. *The New York Times*. Retrieved from https://www.nytimes.com/2003/04/05/nyregion/couple-guilty-of-assault-in-vegan-case.html
Ryan, H. (March 24, 2003). Vegan parents on trial for baby's severe malnutrition. *CNN*. Retrieved from http://www.cnn.com/2003/LAW/03/24/ctv.swinton/
Ryan, H. (March 29, 2003). Vegan mom: "Malnourished" baby was healthy. *CNN*. Retrieved from http://www.cnn.com/2003/LAW/03/29/ctv.swinton/

Case Study 17: Bad Blood
Brandt, A. M. (1978). Racism and research: The case of the Tuskegee syphilis study. *The Hastings Center Report, 8*(6), 21-29. Retrieved from https://dash.harvard.edu/bitstream/handle/1/3372911/brandt_racism.pdf?sequence=1
Clinton, B. (May 16, 1997). Presidential apology. Retrieved from https://www.cdc.gov/tuskegee/clintonp.htm
Heller, J. (July 26, 1972). Syphilis victims in U.S. study went untreated for 40 years. *The New York Times*. Retrieved from

https://www.nytimes.com/1972/07/26/archives/syphilis-victims-in-us-study-went-untreated-for-40-years-syphilis.html

Regan, T. (2004). Human rights. In *Empty cages: Facing the challenge of animal rights*, pp 37-52. Rowman & Littlefield.

The Nuremberg code. (1947). Retrieved from https://history.nih.gov/research/downloads/nuremberg.pdf

Case Study 18: Prison Experiments

Hornblum, A. M. (1999). *Acres of skin: Human experiments at Holmesburg prison*. Routledge.

Munson, R. (2012). Prisoners as test subjects? In *Intervention and reflection: Basic issues in bioethics*, 9th ed. (pp. 118-123 and 138). Wadsworth.

Case Study 19: Huntington's Disease – and Beyond

Ali, A., et al. (2013). The relationship between happiness and intelligence quotient: The contribution of socio-economic and clinical factors. *Psychological Medicine, 43*(6), 1303-1312.

Darwin, K. (2012). An interview with Dr. Nancy Wexler: Discovering the Huntington disease gene. *HD Insights, 3*. Retrieved from http://hdsa.org/wp-content/uploads/2015/02/hd-insights-volume-3.pdf

Savulescu, J. (2001). Procreative beneficence: Why we should select the best children. *Bioethics, 15*(5/6), 413-426.

Sawyer, D., Wexler, A., & Wexler, N. (October 26, 1986). The hardest choice. *60 Minutes*. Retrieved from https://www.cbsnews.com/news/two-sisters-one-horrible-disease/

Case Study 20: The Baby and the Baboon

Pence, G. E. (2008). Using one baby for another. In *Classic cases in medical ethics: Accounts of the cases and issues that define medical ethics* (pp 276-293). 5th ed. McGraw-Hill.

Raspberry, W. (October 31, 1984). Baby Fae's life. *Washington Post*. Retrieved from https://www.washingtonpost.com/archive/politics/1984/10/31/baby-faes-life/51f2b205-e7f3-4483-bc66-ca2c53ba6df2/?noredirect=on&utm_term=.c58dbe2f8de3

Regan, T. (1983). *The case for animal rights*. University of California Press.

Case Study 21: A Hundred Thousand Monkeys

Baicus, A. (August 12, 2012). History of polio vaccination. *World Journal of Virology, 1*(4), 108-114. Retrieved from https://www.ncbi.nlm.nih.gov/pmc/articles/PMC3782271/

Cohen, C. (2001). The factual setting of animal experimentation. In C. Cohen and T. Regan, *The animal rights debate* (pp. 11-16). Rowman & Littlefield.

National Museum of American History. (n.d.). Polio: Two vaccines. Retrieved from https://amhistory.si.edu/polio/virusvaccine/vacraces2.htm

Polio Global Eradication Initiative. (2019). Polio now. Retrieved from http://polioeradication.org/polio-today/polio-now/

Regan, T. (1983). Against the use of animals in science. In *The case for animal rights* (pp. 363-394). University of California Press.

Case Study 22: "One of the Worst Things I Had Ever Done"

The details of Case Study 22 are taken from personal communications with the individuals involved. The names of these individuals have been altered to protect their identity.

Balcombe, J. (2001). Dissection: The scientific case for alternatives. *Journal of Applied Animal Welfare Science, 4*(2), 117-126.

Fears, D. (June 30, 2016). One last U.S. medical school still killed animals to teach surgery. But no more. *The Washington Post*. Retrieved from https://www.washingtonpost.com/news/animalia/wp/2016/06/30/one-last-u-s-medical-school-still-killed-animals-to-teach-surgery-but-no-more/?noredirect=on&utm_term=.9c25405bd304

Case Study 23: A Hopelessly Flawed System?

The details of Case Study 22 are taken from personal communications with the individuals involved. The names of these individuals have been altered to protect their identity.

Case Study 24: Obamacare

111th Congress. (March 23, 2010). *The patient protection and affordable care act*. Retrieved from https://www.govinfo.gov/content/pkg/PLAW-111publ148/pdf/PLAW-111publ148.pdf

Berchick, E. R., Hood., E., & Barnett, J. C. (September 12, 2018). Health insurance coverage in the United States: 2017. Retrieved from https://www.census.gov/library/publications/2018/demo/p60-264.html

Frommer, R. A. (December 29, 2018). Efforts to repeal the Patient Protection and Affordable Care Act. *Medicine in Context, 2*(1). Retrieved from https://medicalreview.columbia.edu/article/affordable-care-act/

Hartman, M., et al. (December 6, 2017). National health care spending in 2016: Spending and enrollment growth slow after initial coverage expansions. *Health Affairs, 37*(1). Retrieved from https://www.healthaffairs.org/doi/10.1377/hlthaff.2017.1299

Mikulic, M. (May 9, 2017). U.S. pharmaceutical industry – statistics & facts. Retrieved from https://www.statista.com/topics/1719/pharmaceutical-industry/

Mikulic, M. (August 27, 2018). Global pharmaceutical industry – statistics & facts. Retrieved from https://www.statista.com/topics/1764/global-pharmaceutical-industry/

Munson, R. (2012). In crisis mode: Background to health care reform. In *Intervention and reflection: Basic issues in bioethics,* 9th ed. (pp. 685-688). Wadsworth.

National Conference of State Legislatures. (2011). The Affordable Care Act: A brief summary. Retrieved from http://www.ncsl.org/research/health/the-affordable-care-act-brief-summary.aspx

Smith, J. C., & Medalia, C. (September 16, 2014). Health insurance coverage in the United States: 2013. Retrieved from https://www.census.gov/library/publications/2014/demo/p60-250.html

United Nations. (2019). World population prospects 2019. Retrieved from https://population.un.org/wpp/Download/Standard/Mortality/

www.ingramcontent.com/pod-product-compliance
Lightning Source LLC
Chambersburg PA
CBHW030118100526
44591CB00009B/437